75 WOK
& STIR-FRY RECIPES

75 WOK
& STIR-FRY RECIPES

SPICY AND AROMATIC DISHES SHOWN STEP BY STEP
IN OVER 350 SUPERB PHOTOGRAPHS

JENNI FLEETWOOD

southwater

This edition is published by Southwater,
an imprint of Anness Publishing Ltd,
108 Great Russell Street,
London WC1B 3NA;
info@anness.com

www.southwaterbooks.com;
www.annesspublishing.com

If you like the images in this book and would like to investigate
using them for publishing, promotions or advertising, please visit
our website www.practicalpictures.com for more information.

A CIP catalogue record for this book
is available from the British Library.

Publisher: Joanna Lorenz
Executive Editor: Joanne Rippin
Photographs: Nicki Dowey, Gus Filgate and Craig Robertson
Additional Recipes: Yasuko Fukuoka and Deh-Ta Hsiung
Designer: Adelle Morris
Production Controller: Pirong Wang

Images on pp8–9 supplied by Travel Ink

NOTES
Bracketed terms are intended for American readers.

For all recipes, quantities are given in both metric and imperial
measures and, where appropriate, in standard cups and spoons.
Follow one set of measures, but not a mixture, because they are
not interchangeable.

Standard spoon and cup measures are level. 1 tsp = 5ml,
1 tbsp = 15ml, 1 cup = 250ml/8fl oz.

Australian standard tablespoons are 20ml. Australian readers
should use 3 tsp in place of 1 tbsp for measuring small quantities.

American pints are 16fl oz/2 cups. American readers should use
20fl oz/2.5 cups in place of 1 pint when measuring liquids.

Electric oven temperatures in this book are for conventional ovens.
When using a fan oven, the temperature will probably need to be
reduced by about 10–20°C/20–40°F. Since ovens vary, you should
check with your manufacturer's instruction book for guidance.

The nutritional analysis given for each recipe is calculated per
portion (i.e. serving or item), unless otherwise stated. If the recipe
gives a range, such as Serves 4–6, then the nutritional analysis will
be for the smaller portion size, i.e. 6 servings. The analysis does not
include optional ingredients, such as salt added to taste.

Medium (US large) eggs are used unless otherwise stated.

Main front cover image shows Sweet and Sour Pork – for recipe,
see page 89.

CONTENTS

INTRODUCTION

Perhaps the most ancient cooking vessel in the world, the wok is an amazingly versatile implement, in which you can stir-fry, deep-fry, sauté, steam and simmer. It makes short work of soups and sauces, and is as handy for poaching pears as it is for braising beef.

When it comes to design, the wok is a hugely effective cooking vessel. Heat radiates up the sides to produce a pan that cooks fast and efficiently. Its depth gives plenty of room for tossing and turning without fallout, and the sloping sides ensure that the food always returns to the narrow base, where the heat is most intense.

Wok sales have rocketed in recent years. In the 1960s and 70s, a wok was something of a novelty, often bought in a burst of enthusiasm after a visit to a Chinese restaurant, then left to rust at the back of a kitchen cupboard. And rust they did, largely because people didn't know how to look after them. Part of the problem was the fact that most of the woks on sale were constructed of carbon steel. This was – and still is – an excellent material, but it needs an initial treatment to develop a non-stick, rust-resistant surface.

Fortunately, there were enough fans of this excellent pan to spread the word, and the wok gradually gained ground. It was still used mainly for Chinese food only, however, and filled the same sort of specialist slot as the fondue pot or

Below: Ingredients for a stir-fry should be the freshest available to maximize the flavour and crispness.

Left: Kaffir lime leaves add a wonderful aroma to stir-fries.

waffle iron. Fusion food changed all that. When chefs no longer viewed each nation's cuisine as sacrosanct, and started inventing new dishes that combined ingredients from several sources, they did us all a favour. The wok stopped being used solely for sweet and sour pork, and came to be seen as a practical pan for all sorts of dishes.

Around the same time, the pattern of everyday life was changing. People weren't just eating out more: they were adopting more flexible eating habits. Often there wasn't enough time to cook an elaborate meal, so something that could be whizzed up in a wok was absolutely ideal. When it became apparent that this utensil was a fixture, rather than a short-lived culinary craze, manufacturers started producing woks in different materials, including non-stick ones that needed very little aftercare or special treatment. Flat-based versions were developed for use on modern electric stoves, the first electric appliances appeared, and more and more cookbooks catered for the quick and convenient style of cooking the wok promised.

Throughout all this, the wok delivered, and is still delivering. Today, it is its role

in promoting healthy eating that is catching the public imagination. What the wok does extremely well is to cook a sizeable quantity of vegetables with a small amount of protein and the minimum of fat. When carbohydrate is added, in the form of noodles or rice, you have a well-balanced dish that any nutritionist would approve of. Deep-frying doesn't score a lot of brownie points in the health stakes, but if the oil is hot enough, the outer surface will be sealed immediately after the food is immersed, and the amount of oil absorbed will be limited. Steaming, however, gets a gold star. This is one of the healthiest ways to cook, since no additional fat is needed, the natural flavour of the food is preserved, and colours remain bright and true.

When you own a wok, you will find yourself discovering new uses for it, whether cooking spaghetti sauce, braising chicken portions, simmering fruit in syrup, making risotto, steaming asparagus or smoking salmon. It may not be the only pot you'll ever need, but it will be the one you use most often.

Right: The wok is superb for deep-frying, as it seals and crisps the coating very quickly, leaving the filling moist and succulent, as in these tuna rolls.

Below: A sweet and hot chilli sauce is the perfect accompaniment to delicious crispy appetizers fried in the wok.

THE UNIVERSAL WOK

Left: Ready-cooked meals are laid out in a dazzling variety in a market stall in Bangkok. The food will be taken home and quickly heated up in a wok.

The wok has been the utensil of choice throughout Asia for thousands of years. It was originally developed in China as a fast and efficient way of cooking over wood or charcoal. Fuel was scarce and expensive, so it made sense to cook food fast in just one pan. The first woks were made of hammered iron. They had rounded bases and looked like inverted straw hats of the type worn by peasant farmers. The conical shape wasn't a drawback when the wok was wedged among logs on an open fire or seated on the well of a primitive stove. In fact, it was a positive advantage, since oil in the narrow base heated rapidly and the pan became extremely hot as flames licked up the thin slanted sides. Small pieces of food cooked very quickly and evenly, provided they were kept on the move. If a liquid was heated in the wok, and a bamboo steamer set on top, the basket could be used for steaming. This was another way of making the most of available fuel, especially when steamers were stacked on top of each other.

Right: Men cook chapattis in a huge bubbling wok, ready for a family celebration in New Delhi.

WOKS BECOME WIDESPREAD

Use of the wok started to spread. In Japan it became known as the *chukanabe*, in Thailand it was dubbed the *kata* and in India, a long-handled version was the forerunner of the *karahi*. When introduced to Indonesia, the wok was christened the *wadjang*. Filipinos liked the wok so much they developed two versions: the large *kawa* and the smaller *kawali*.

Wherever the wok is used, the basic design is the same, but what is cooked in it is not. Mongolian cooks use their woks for heating milk and making yak butter tea; the Japanese make tempura in theirs and Indians use a karahi for braising foods. In Malaysia, where a wok is called a *kuali*, the pan plays a significant role in the Kadazan wedding ceremony. The bridal pair are seated facing each other and a *kuali*, brimming with rice, is placed before them to signify that they will never go hungry.

THE TRAVELLING WOK

Asians who emigrated to Europe, America and elsewhere took their woks with them. Often these became family heirlooms, and as they passed from one generation to the next, so too did favourite family recipes. There's a lovely theory that the metal in a wok holds the memory of everything that has ever been cooked in it, so these grand old woks, blackened and battered but still efficient, are imprinted with decades of delicious meals.

Left: A large quantity of soy sauce simmers away in a huge, mechanically stirred wok, in Chengdu, China.

others are flat-based so that they sit safely on electric stoves. They come in a variety of materials and sizes, from 25cm/10in to supersized 90cm/36in commercial models. You can even buy a wok that fits on a kettle barbecue, so you can stir-fry outside as the sun sets.

For the average family of three or four, the standard 36cm/14in wok is ideal. Even the Aga, the classic cooking range, now incorporates a twin-flamed wok burner in many of its models. This is proof, perhaps, that the wok is here to stay, and not just for stir-fries and other Asian dishes.

HOW THE WOK WORKS

For a wok to work efficiently, it must be capable of becoming very hot very quickly, but should cool down rapidly when removed from the heat so that the food does not continue to cook, and go past the point of perfection. The original cast-iron woks did both these jobs well but were very heavy, so when thin carbon steel came along, it was widely welcomed as an alternative.

Carbon steel is light but durable, and conducts heat quickly and evenly. Despite the fact that there are now many more types of wok on the market, carbon steel is still reckoned to give the best results. If it is properly "seasoned", a carbon steel wok will quickly develop its own natural non-stick surface that will last if cared for. However, for easy care, some people prefer a wok made of stainless steel or a modern alloy such as spun aluminium and titanium, with a non-stick coating.

A WORLDWIDE SUCCESS

Today the wok is an essential utensil in kitchens all over the globe, and there are dozens of variations on the theme, including electric versions. Some woks have the traditional rounded base;

Right: Thailand is famous for its street food. Here a man cooks pad thai noodles in Bangkok.

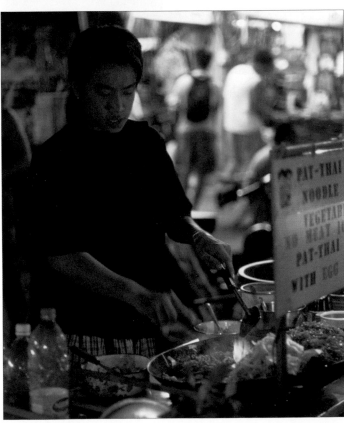

WOKS, TOOLS AND ACCESSORIES

Left: Woks come in many different shapes and sizes and can be used to cook meals for one or for many.

using a steel wok over time, but you will gain by having an easy-care utensil that will give you very satisfactory results. It is essential to use a non-stick pan if you are cooking acidic foods such as fruits, which would discolour in a steel wok.

SIZE AND SHAPE

An average 36cm/14in wok is ideal for most kitchens, and will sit comfortably on the average burner. If you have a large family, or intend to cook whole fish on a regular basis, choose a 40cm/16in model. Whether you buy a round-based wok or a flat-based one depends on the type of stove you have, as well as your personal preference. Purists plump for round-based woks, claiming the shape gives perfect results, as the area of intense heat is very small and the upward slope uninterrupted. However, a round-based wok will wobble if placed on an electric stove. To stabilize it, you would have to use a wok stand or ring, but the round base could still reflect heat back and damage the electric

Choosing a wok isn't difficult. There are dozens of versions on the market, from conventional carbon steel and stainless steel models to modern non-stick woks that are sold solo or in gift packs with tools and even serving bowls. If you're a serious cook who likes the classical approach, begin your search at a large Asian food store, where you can examine traditional carbon steel woks in a range of shapes and sizes, hefting them in your hands to find the weight and size that suits. If you buy a good quality pan and season it properly, it will give you years of excellent service, and will actually improve with age. A cheaper wok may well have to be replaced after a year or so. Avoid very cheap woks, as they may rust despite your best efforts, or develop hot spots.

NON-STICK WOKS

If you prefer a non-stick wok, look for one made from reinforced titanium, which is guaranteed against scratching and can safely be washed in the dishwasher. You won't get the patina and flavour build-up that comes with

Below: A double-handled wok is ideal for using as a serving dish as well as a cooking vessel.

*Above:
A Chinese
cleaver is finely
balanced.*

element. So, for electric stoves, or any stove with a level cooking surface, flat-based woks are best. If you have a gas stove, you can use either style of wok. You probably won't need a wok ring, but if you do, make sure that the wok sits down snugly, so that it is close to the heat source.

Both single-handled woks and twin-handled Cantonese woks are available. The single-handed wok is reckoned to be best for stir-frying, while the twin is more stable and is recommended for deep-frying, steaming and braising. Some woks offer you both features by giving you a 30cm/12in long handle matched with a short, round "helper" handle on the opposite side so that the wok can easily be moved from stove to table. Whichever type you buy, get a domed lid, so that you can use your wok for steaming or braising.

ELECTRIC WOK

The electric wok doesn't get quite as hot as a carbon steel wok over high heat, but is efficient, convenient and very good for cooking braised dishes and risotto. It can make a meal in moments, busy cooks like it because it leaves the stove free for other items, and others value its stability and the fact that the heat is thermostatically

Below: An electric wok is ideal for braising and slow cooking.

controlled. Electric woks come in various sizes but all are similar in design, with a heat element recessed in the stay-cool base. The wok that sits securely on the base will inevitably have a non-stick coating, but may need to be given a token seasoning before being used for the first time. The handbook will give instructions on how this is to be done – usually it merely means coating the wok with oil and heating it for 5 minutes, then wiping it clean and letting it cool down.

TOOLS AND ACCESSORIES

It isn't necessary to buy special tools for wok cooking, but there are a few items that will prove useful.

Cleavers and Knives

Cutting meat and vegetables for stir-frying so that the maximum surface area is exposed to the heat is quite an art, and Chinese cooks swear that the best tool for the job is a cleaver. This short-handled implement has a large, flat blade that can be used to cut everything from paper-thin vegetable slices to meat on the bone. When the blade is held flat, it can be used like a spatula, to transport the prepared food to the wok. Cleavers come in several sizes and weights. Number one is the heaviest and resembles a chopper more than a knife. Its 23cm/9in long blade is 10cm/4in wide, and is mainly used for

slicing. The medium weight number two cleaver is the most popular choice for general kitchen use. It is used for both slicing and chopping. The back of the blade is ideal for pounding meat to tenderize it, and the flat surface can be used to crush garlic or ginger. Good quality kitchen knives can be used instead of a cleaver. A 10cm/4in paring knife and a 20cm/8in cook's knife will be the most useful sizes. It is vital to keep blades sharp, either by using a steel or a stone.

Mortar and Pestle

South-east Asian cooks like to use their woks for making quick curries. These depend for their flavour on curry pastes that are freshly made using ingredients like galangal, garlic and lemon grass. A granite mortar is best for this purpose, since the rough surface amplifies the pounding action of the pestle and also helps to grip the ingredients so they do not escape from the bowl. Buy a mortar that measures at least 18cm/7in across. This is sufficient for mixtures of up to 450ml/¾ pint/scant 2 cups.

Draining or Steaming Rack

Most woks, whether standard or electric, come with a rainbow-shaped metal rack that clips on to the rim. This item, sometimes called a tempura rack, is useful when deep-frying. As items cook, they can be set to drain on the rack. Surplus oil will drip back into the pan, and the drained foods can be moved to a piece of kitchen paper when the rack is full. The rack can also be used for steaming, and is particularly useful in an electric wok.

Spatulas and Scoops

It is useful to have at least two wooden spatulas for stir-frying, preferably with a rounded side that follows the contours of the wok. Another useful implement is the *charn*, a long-handled spatula shaped like a shovel, which makes it easy to scoop and toss foods that are being stir-fried. If you use a charn in a non-stick pan, take care not to scratch the surface.

Ladle

You will need a ladle for spooning soups or other liquids out of the wok. Choose one with a deep bowl. Although black nylon ladles are recommended for non-stick woks, they do scorch easily, so stainless steel ladles are a better bet. Some ladles have graduated markings inside that indicate how much liquid they contain. This is useful when you need to spoon out a specific quantity of stock. If your ladle is not marked in this

Below: You may need a wok ring on your stove top to keep the wok steady.

Above: Essential wok tools include a dome-shaped lid, wooden or bamboo chopsticks, a long-handled spatula and a large ladle.

way, measure the liquid it holds by filling it with water and spooning this into a measuring jug (cup). Making a note of the amount for future reference will help you when you are following a recipe that specifies a particular amount of liquid to be removed from the wok.

Chopsticks

If you wander through an Asian street market you will sometimes see food being stirred in giant woks with extra-long chopsticks. These are ideal for the dextrous, but tongs or two spatulas can be used instead.

Skimmers

These are long handled utensils with wire or bamboo scoops at one end. These can be cup- or saucer-shaped and are used to fish food out of hot oil or stock. Saucer-shaped skimmers are also called spiders, since they resemble circular webs.

Wok Ring

This circular metal stand gives stability to a round-based wok when used on an electric or gas stove. The rings come in several sizes and designs. The most common ones look like crumpet rings or cookie cutters, and consist of solid metal that may be punched with ventilation holes. Thick wire stands are also available, and these are recommended for gas stoves. It is important to buy a ring that supports your wok securely while allowing it to be as close to the heat source as possible without putting out the flame. If your wok has a flat base you won't need a ring. If you intend using a wok ring on an electric stove, check with the manufacturer, as this practice can damage the element.

Steamers

Steaming is one of the healthiest ways of cooking, since no fat is required and the natural flavour of the food is preserved. A wok is ideal for this purpose, since its shape gives you a large surface area of water to turn into steam. There are several ways of steaming in a wok. For just a few items, you can use the semicircular rack that clips on to the side of the pan.

Left: A perforated metal scoop and a traditional wire skimmer.

Above: Racks can be clipped to the side of a wok to drain deep-fried food on.

Alternatively, you can place items to be steamed on a heatproof plate, provided you raise the plate above the surface of the water or stock by means of a trivet or upturned cup. You can also steam items by the Chinese method, using stackable bamboo baskets. An expanding metal steamer will also work well, but take care that the feet do not scratch the surface of the wok if it has a non-stick coating. Whichever means you use, you will need to trap the steam somehow, either by fitting a domed lid over the wok, or making sure the steamer itself is tightly covered.

Preparing a Steamer

Before you use a bamboo steamer for the first time, scrub it well, using a mild soap if you like, then rinse it thoroughly, Place the wet steamer over boiling water in a wok. Steam it empty for at least 10 minutes, then leave to air dry. Store in a well-ventilated place.

Bamboo Steamers

Although stainless-steel steamers are regarded as being more hygienic, natural bamboo steamers do an excellent job, since the material allows steam to circulate freely with only minimal condensation. The steamer baskets can be bought singly or in sets and come in various sizes. Standard steamers have a diameter of 25cm/10in and are about 15cm/6in tall. This is the ideal size for a 36cm/14in wok. When the basket is in use, there should be at least 5cm/2in space between it and the side of the wok. Steamers can be stacked.

Left: A stack of steamers increases the amount of food you can cook at one time.

Seasoning a Wok

First wash the wok thoroughly in warm water and detergent to remove any preservative coating. Rinse, shake off the excess water, then place the wok over low heat to dry. Add a little cooking oil (not olive oil) and, using kitchen paper, wipe the pan to coat it evenly. Take care not to burn yourself. Heat gently for 10–12 minutes, then wipe off the oil with clean kitchen paper. Don't be alarmed when it blackens – this is perfectly natural. Repeat the process for as long as it takes for the paper to come away clean, by which time the wok itself will have darkened. The more it is used, the better the wok's natural non-stick coating will become and the easier it will be to clean. If a wok should rust – perhaps because it has been put away wet or abandoned in a cupboard for months – it should be rubbed down with wire wool or fine sandpaper and then seasoned again. A cast iron or carbon steel wok is less likely to rust if it is oiled lightly before being stored.

Cleaning a Wok

A properly seasoned wok should never be washed with detergent. Remove any food that sticks to the surface, then wash the wok in hot water. Dry thoroughly by placing the wok over the heat for a few minutes. Leave to cool, then rub a little oil into the surface.

FISH AND SHELLFISH

Given the versatility of the wok, there's literally no end to the ingredients that can be cooked in it. However, there are some items that lend themselves particularly well to stir-frying, steaming and braising. Inevitably, these are ingredients that cook quickly, a prime example of which is fish and seafood. Fish can be cooked in a wok in various ways. The more robust types, such as cod, haddock and halibut, can be cut into bitesize portions and stir-fried. Stir-frying is also an excellent way of cooking prawns (shrimp) and scallops.

Right:
Fish, such
as sea bass,
are perfect for
cooking whole in
the wok.

COD AND HADDOCK

White fish such as cod is a great choice for soups and fish curries. Add the pearly white cubes to the liquid in the wok towards the end of cooking so that they keep their shape. They will be ready to eat in a couple of minutes. Cod and haddock can also be steamed. Haddock has a more delicate flavour and softer texture. This fish is a good choice for deep-frying. Dip pieces in batter before adding them to hot oil.

HALIBUT

A delicious flatfish, halibut has a fine, meaty texture. For steaming whole, choose the small variety, often called chicken halibut, or opt for steaks cut

Below: Firm-fleshed, white fish, such as cod and haddock, are ideal for cooking as steaks or in bite-sized pieces.

from the middle. Halibut is robust enough to hold its own against spicy flavours and tastes great with tomatoes in a curry.

PRAWNS

The most common shellfish ingredient in Asian cooking, prawns – or shrimp, as they are known in the US – are one of the finest ingredients for stir-frying, steaming or deep-frying, since they require very little time to cook. Larger varieties such as tiger prawns are particularly good. When buying prawns in the shell, allow about 300g/11oz per serving, as there is a lot of wastage.

SALMON

Although salmon can be cooked in a variety of ways, it is particularly good steamed in a bamboo basket. Flaked salmon makes great fish cakes.

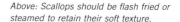

Above: Scallops should be flash fried or steamed to retain their soft texture.

SCALLOPS

These tender molluscs are delectable but very delicate, so take care not to overcook them. Scallops are delicious steamed with ginger and spring onions (scallions), or try them seared and served on wilted pak choi (boy choy).

SEA BASS

Fish such as sea bass can be steamed whole in the wok. Choose a fish that weighs about 450g/1lb for two people. Strong flavours such as ginger, garlic, soy sauce and lemon grass work well with sea bass.

SQUID

For stir-frying, slit the body of the squid from top to bottom and turn it inside out. Flatten it, then score the flesh with a knife to make a criss-cross pattern. Cut lengthwise into ribbons. These will curl when stir-fried.

MEAT AND POULTRY

Only the tenderest cuts of meat are suitable for wok cooking, especially if they are to be stir-fried. Traditional Asian recipes favour chicken, duck and pork, but there is no reason to limit yourself to these choices. Beef, lamb and even ostrich taste great when cooked in the wok.

BEEF

Steak is ideal for stir-frying, whether you choose fillet (tenderloin), rump (round) or sirloin. Look for deep red meat with a light marbling of fat. If a recipe requires beef to be very thinly sliced, place it in the freezer for about half an hour beforehand. For stir-fries, strips of beef are often marinated in a mixture that includes soy sauce and oil. When cooking, have the wok very hot, add a few strips at a time, and move them to the sides of the wok before adding more. If too much meat is added to the wok at the same time, the temperature will drop and the strips of beef will simply stew in the liquid that accumulates during cooking.

CHICKEN

Tender breast portions or fillets are perfect for stir-frying. If thin strips of chicken are required, flatten the breast fillets by placing them between two sheets of clear film (plastic wrap) and beating them lightly but firmly with a rolling pin.

Below: Chicken, when flattened and cut into thin strips, is ideal for stir-fries.

Left: Pork is a great favourite in Chinese and Asian dishes.

DUCK

In China and Thailand, duck is sometimes cooked whole, but is more often thinly sliced and stir-fried, or cubed and used to make a spicy curry. Most of the meat on a duck is concentrated in the breast, so, despite

Below: Lamb is not used in the Far East but makes a great wok ingredient.

Below: Duck is tender and full of flavour, and ideal for fast wok cooking.

Right: The best cuts of beef are superb for fast frying, while cheaper cuts can be slow-cooked to tenderize.

the cost, it can be more practical to buy breast portions instead of whole birds. Duck breasts can be steamed in a wok, then sliced, moistened with a little of the stock from the steamer and served in a salad.

LAMB

Choose lean leg of lamb for stir-frying, or lamb fillet (tenderloin), which is cut from the middle of the neck. The meat should be firm and pink. The paler the meat, the younger the lamb. To make medallions of lamb, cut the fillet into thin, even slices. These can be stir-fried or braised in the wok. Alternatively, cut the lamb into strips. Soy sauce and lamb go well together and marinating lamb in it for 2–3 hours before frying imparts the most wonderful flavour.

PORK

Fillet (tenderloin) is the most tender cut and is relatively inexpensive, given the fact that it consists of solid meat with very little wastage. Choose fillets that are pale pink all over, with no areas of discoloration. The flesh should be fairly firm, never flaccid, and slightly moist to the touch.

To prepare pork fillet, first pull away the membrane that surrounds the meat and remove any fat. Using a sharp knife, slice away the tendon and sinew, which looks like a tougher strip of membrane. For stir-frying, slice pork fillet in neat, even strips; for braising, opt for medallions, cut on the diagonal.

VEGETABLES AND AROMATICS

When you cook vegetables and aromatics in a wok, the aim is to retain maximum flavour and texture. The flavour must be there in the first place, so shopping carefully is the first step towards good cooking. Buy vegetables at the peak of condition, preferably from a farmer's market or greengrocer that sources produce locally, rather than buying shrink-wrapped items that have travelled great distances between soil and superstore. The best vegetables for wok cooking are those that stay crisp after stir-frying.

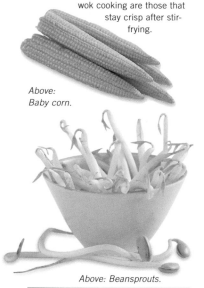

Above:
Baby corn.

Above: Beansprouts.

Banana Leaves

Not strictly an ingredient, these large, pliable leaves are used in Thai cooking in particular, to wrap food for steaming in the wok. The leaves impart a mild smoky flavour to the food.

BABY CORN

These miniature corn cobs are good for stir-frying, either whole or sliced in half through their length. The shape and colour create interest and they keep their crunch when cooked.

BEANSPROUTS

Highly nutritious, beansprouts are delicious in stir-fries. They are highly perishable, so make sure they are absolutely fresh and use them as soon as possible after you purchase them.

CHINESE LEAVES

This sweet-tasting green vegetable is often mistaken for a type of lettuce but is actually a brassica, which accounts for its American name, "Chinese cabbage". An excellent salad ingredient, when stir-fried, the white stalk stays crisp and provides a contrast to the softer texture of the leaves. To prepare, remove any discoloured or damaged leaves, trim the root, then slice the head across into thin shreds. Chinese leaves are sometimes used to make a bed in a bamboo steamer for cooking pieces of fish or meat.

MANGETOUT

Americans call these "snow peas" but the French word, which means "eat all", describes them better, since the entire pod is consumed.

PEPPERS

Sweet "bell" peppers are ideal ingredients for the wok, contributing colour as well as flavour. When cooked quickly they retain some crunch and are delightfully juicy. To prepare a pepper, make an incision all the way around the stem-end. Pull off the lid and, with any luck, the core and seeds will come away too. Cut the pepper in half, remove any remaining seeds and

Left: Chinese leaves.

hard ribs, then dice the flesh or cut it into neat slices. Slice the flesh off the lid too.

PAK CHOI

Known by various names, including "bok choy" and "Chinese chard", this member of the cabbage family is distinguished by its fat white stems. Many people think the stalks taste even better than the glossy green leaves, but both are great steamed or in a stir-fry. The stems take slightly longer to cook than the leaves, so start them first.

Below: Pak choi.

MOOLI

A long white root also known as "daikon" used as a crisp, sharp, cool addition to a salad – or cooked. Whether steamed or fried, it retains its crisp texture, but develops a sweeter flavour.

MUSHROOMS

All mushrooms cook quickly and are great for the wok. Fresh shiitake and oyster mushrooms are readily available and are excellent in stir-fries, but button (white) mushrooms can be used instead. Dried mushrooms add an intense flavour. Soak them in warm

Above: Mooli.

Above: Mushrooms.

water for 30 minutes, then lift them out of the soaking water, remove the stems and slice or chop the caps. Strain the soaking water and add it to stocks or soups when needed.

SPRING ONIONS

Many wok recipes call for spring onions (scallions) to be stir-fried at the start of cooking. Regular onions or shallots can be used instead. The purpose of using these aromatic vegetables is to give overall depth of flavour, so they should be finely diced or sliced so that they blend with other ingredients and do not physically dominate the dish.

SEAWEED

There are several types of edible seaweed, including kombu, nori, wakame and hijiki. Their main function in wok cooking is to flavour stocks, soups and simmered dishes.

WATER CHESTNUTS

Much more readily available canned than fresh, water chestnuts, and the similar bamboo shoots are both very good in stir-fries, so keep some in the storecupboard at all times. Water chestnuts add a wonderful crisp texture and nutty flavour.

CHILLIES

These fiery peppers are often used in curries and spicy stir-fries. There are many varieties in different strengths, and even chillies from the same plant can vary in intensity, so treat them with caution. When preparing chillies, protect yourself from the capsaicin they contain by wearing gloves, or wash your hands thoroughly with soap afterwards to prevent chilli-burn. To prepare chillies, slit them and scrape out the seeds and pith. Most of the heat is in the seeds, so add them only if you want a very spicy result. If you grind chillies to make a curry paste, avoid standing with your face directly over the mortar.

GALANGAL

This looks like ginger but can be distinguished by its finger-like sprouts. When young, these are pale pink in colour and taste almost lemony. As the plant matures, the skin thickens and the creamy skin turns pale gold. The flavour is now quite peppery. Galangal is used in the same way as ginger and is often incorporated in pastes.

GARLIC

The universal aromatic, garlic is great for stir-frying but burns easily at the very high temperatures achieved in the wok. It is best to cook it briefly or add with other vegetables. Garlic can be crushed easily with a cleaver.

Left: Galangal.

Above: Seaweed.

Below: Ginger.

GINGER

A favourite ingredient in Asian cooking traditions, ginger adds a wonderful warmth and flavour to savoury and sweet foods. Peel off the skin and either chop or grate the flesh.

LEMON GRASS

The distinctive citrus flavour of this plant makes it a favourite ingredient in stir-fries or curry pastes. Lemon grass stalks are sold in bundles. To prepare, peel away and discard the fibrous layers surrounding each stalk. Only the tenderest part of the stalk – the bottom 10–15cm/4–6in – is suitable for stir-frying. It can either be sliced or pounded into a paste. Don't discard offcuts: add them to water used for steaming fish or chicken in the wok. Lemon grass can be bought dried, but this doesn't work so well in stir fries.

Left: Lemon grass.

RICE

Many of the savoury dishes cooked in a wok either incorporate rice or are served with rice. Fried rice is a wok standard, but the pan can also be used to make a pilaff or a risotto.

THAI JASMINE RICE

This delicately scented long grain rice is the ideal accompaniment for stir-fries and similar dishes and is also a good choice for making fried rice. The uncooked grains are translucent and become fluffy and white when boiled. The flavour is slightly nutty. Fried rice often includes vegetables such as shredded pak choi (bok choy) or spring greens (collards), together with aromatic flavourings such as garlic and chilli. In vegetarian versions, coconut or cashew nuts are favourite additions. Protein can be added in the form of strips of omelette, chicken, beef or pork or prawns (shrimp).

BASMATI RICE

For Indian cooking and fusion food, basmati is the obvious choice. This long grain rice lives up to its Hindi name, which translates as "the fragrant one". The grains are long and slender and have very good texture. Basmati is the best type of rice to use for a pilaff, and a wok with a tight-fitting lid is an ideal pan for the task.

RISOTTO RICE

Italians recommend using a heavy pan for making risotto, but maybe that's because they didn't invent the wok. The latter works extremely well, the only

Above: Risotto rice.

drawback being that the large surface area makes for more rapid evaporation of the liquid added to the rice, so it is particularly important to stir the mixture constantly and check the rice frequently to prevent it from becoming overcooked. You may also need to add slightly more liquid than the amount listed in a recipe, so make sure you have some

spare. When the rice is creamy, but the grains retain a hint of firmness at the centre, the risotto is ready.

Long grain rice isn't suitable for making risotto. What is needed is a comparatively large, plump short grain with a high proportion of starch. As the rice cooks, the rice dissolves in the stock that is constantly added to give the finished dish a creamy texture. There are several varieties of risotto rice. Carnaroli and Vialone Nano give excellent results. The starchy outer layer of the grain dissolves, but the centre retains enough "bite" to provide the perfect contrast. Arborio also works well but contains more amylopectin than the other two varieties, so has a tendency to become pappy if overcooked. Removing the risotto from the heat before it is fully cooked, and leaving it to stand, covered, for 4–5 minutes, overcomes this drawback.

Serving Rice Safely

Serve rice as soon as it is cooked, if possible. Never keep it warm for long periods or food poisoning might result. The danger comes from *bacillus cereus*, which is often present in uncooked rice. If the rice is boiled and served straight away there is little risk, but if cooked rice is left to stand at room temperature, or kept warm for a long period, any toxic spores present may multiply. If you intend using cooked rice in a salad, it is important to cool it quickly and keep it covered in the refrigerator until required. If you reheat rice, don't just warm it; it must be piping hot right through.

Below: Thai jasmine rice.

Below: Basmati rice.

NOODLES AND WRAPPERS

In Asia, where the wok originated, noodles are an integral part of the diet, served in soups, salads, stir-fries and sweet dishes. They are a symbol of longevity in China and are often on the menu at birthday parties, weddings and wakes. Although noodles are traditionally used with wok dishes, there's nothing to stop you substituting pasta if you prefer.

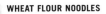

Above: Fine rice noodles.

Noodles suitable for wok cooking are usually made from wheat flour or rice flour, but can also be based on mung beans, buckwheat, seaweed or more exotic ingredients. They generally come in bundles, bound by slips of paper or formed into nests, and can be fresh, semi-cooked or dried. Most noodles taste fairly bland, which makes them a good vehicle for spicy food. Children love to slurp them in soup, workers value them as fast food and their digestibility makes them a good choice for anyone. They can be served on their own, with a simple sauce, or form part of an elaborate dish. Noodle paste is also used to make wrappers for spring rolls and other deep-fried treats.

Below: Egg noodles are available in both fresh and dried form.

EGG NOODLES

Like Italian pasta, Asian wheat noodles can be plain or enriched with egg. In China, both types are available, but egg noodles (easy to spot at the supermarket because they are usually labelled as such) are those with which people in the West are most familiar. Japanese egg noodles are called *ramen*.

WHEAT FLOUR NOODLES

Plain wheat noodles go by various names. In Japan they are called *udon*. They come in several widths; *somen* being a slim type similar to the Korean *somyen*. Wheat

Above: Rice stick noodles.

noodles need to be boiled briefly before use. Fresh ones will often be ready in less than 1 minute; dried noodles take 3–5 minutes. Exact timing depends on the type, the thickness and whether the noodles will be mixed with other ingredients and cooked for a while longer. Some types can be added straight to the wok. See individual recipes for more information.

RICE FLOUR NOODLES

Pre-cooking is part of the process of making rice noodles, so they need even less preparation than wheat noodles. Before use, just soak them in hot water for 5–10 minutes or for as long as it takes for the strands to become soft. If you intend to fry them, this step can be skipped, but use the very thin noodles rather than the thicker rice sticks.

BUCKWHEAT AND CELLOPHANE NOODLES

Soba are Japanese noodles made from buckwheat with wheat flour to give elasticity. They have an earthy flavour. *Soba* are often served cold, with enough sauce to coat the strands but not swamp the taste. Cook them in boiling water until tender. Made from mung beans,

cellophane noodles (also sold as glass, jelly or bean thread noodles) are transparent when cooked and look pretty in a salad or stir-fry.

WRAPPERS

Simple snacks such as spring rolls, wontons, tung tong and rice paper parcels are easy to deep-fry in the wok, and because of the shape of the pan, you need less oil than in a conventional deep-fat fryer. Square, rectangular and round wrappers are available in packets from Asian food stores. Like noodles, wrappers are made from either rice or from wheat, or wheat mixed with egg.

Below: Square wonton wrappers.

Below: Japanese somen noodles are wheat-based.

Oils and Fats

Although the design of a wok means that oil is the ingredient you need least of – unless you are deep-frying – the type you use is important because of the high temperatures involved.

CORN OIL

Extracted from the germ of the corn kernel, this polyunsaturated oil is almost tasteless, although it can have a discernible odour. It is very good for both stir-frying and deep-fat frying since it can withstand high heat without reaching smoking point.

GROUNDNUT OIL

Also known as peanut oil, this is ideal for use in the wok, as it reaches a high temperature without smoking and has a neutral flavour that won't mask the taste of the food. Like olive oil, groundnut oil is monounsaturated, although it does contain a slightly higher percentage of saturated fat than corn or sunflower oil. Some people are allergic to groundnut oil, so inform guests if you have used it for cooking.

Below: sunflower oil (left); groundnut oil (middle); olive oil (right).

LARD

Although this animal fat is no longer widely used for frying in the West, because of the health implications, it remains a common cooking medium in parts of China. The disadvantage of using lard, other than the fact that it is a saturated fat, is that it is often strongly flavoured.

OLIVE OIL

This type of oil is never used for Asian cooking. The flavour simply doesn't go with Asian ingredients. You can use it in the wok for Mediterranean-type dishes, but it is not ideal for frying as it burns at a low temperature

RAPESEED (CANOLA) OIL

This monounsaturated oil is particularly popular in North America. It is pale gold in colour and has a mild flavour and aroma. The smoking point is not quite as high as for corn oil, but the refined oil is regarded as a good choice for stir-frying and deep-frying.

SESAME OIL

Light sesame oil can be used for frying, but the dark type made from roasted sesame seeds is largely used for flavouring. It has a nutty taste, which becomes more pronounced if the oil is warmed. It mustn't be allowed to get too hot, though, or it will burn. A few drops of sesame oil are often added to soup, noodles or a stir-fry before serving.

SUNFLOWER OIL

Another much-used polyunsaturated oil, this has a mild flavour. With a smoking point that rivals that of corn oil and groundnut oil, it is a very good choice for wok cooking.

Above: Sesame oil (top); chilli oil (bottom). These oils are used to flavour dishes rather than as a frying medium.

WOK OIL

This product, specially developed for the wok, combines soya and sesame oils and is flavoured with ginger, garlic and pepper. It's an expensive way to start a stir-fry, but gives good results and is convenient if you have little time.

Butter

When making a typical Asian stir-fry in your wok, you need the fat to be very hot so that the food is instantly seared. Butter won't work for this as it burns at high temperatures, becoming blackened and unpleasant tasting. However, if you are using your wok as a sauté pan, perhaps for a risotto or similar dish, there's no reason why you can't benefit from the delicious flavour of butter. Using half butter and half oil is a good compromise, since the oil enables the butter to withstand higher temperatures.

TOFU, SOYA, AND VEGETABLE PROTEINS

An inexpensive protein food, tofu is made from soya beans, and was invented by the Chinese. It is now widely used throughout the world as an alternative to fish and meat. When it comes to wok cooking, tofu and similar products score on several fronts. They are highly nutritious, easy to use and need little or no cooking. Although most forms are very bland, they take on surrounding flavours, so are useful for adding bulk while boosting food values. Tofu is low in fat and cholesterol-free.

SILKEN TOFU

This white product is the softest, most delicate form of tofu. A creamy version comes in tubs and can be used for dips or desserts, including a non-dairy ice cream. The slightly firmer type of silken tofu comes in cubes, which break down very easily, so must be handled gently. If you use silken tofu cubes in a stir-fry, add them right at the end and don't toss the mixture too vigorously.

FIRM TOFU

This lightly pressed product is sold in cakes or blocks, either submerged in water or vacuum-packed, and can be cubed or sliced. It makes a good addition to a stir-fry, especially if it is marinated in soy sauce or tamari with strong flavours such as

Right: Deep-fried tofu. Below: Fresh firm tofu.

ginger, garlic or fermented black beans. Firm tofu also tastes good in a Thai-style curry.

FRIED TOFU

At first glance, this doesn't look much like tofu. Slice the nut-brown block, however, and the white interior is exposed. The outer colour is the result of deep-frying in vegetable oil, a process than not only adds flavour, but also makes the tofu more robust. Fried tofu won't break down when cooked, whether you stir-fry it or braise the chunks in a sauce.

GLUTEN

This is precisely what it says it is – gluten derived from wheat flour – which can be treated to masquerade as meat, poultry or fish. Flavoured, pre-cooked gluten comes in cans. The contents only need to be heated before being served.

TEMPEH

To make this Indonesian speciality, whole soya beans are

Left: Pressed fried tofu.

fermented with a cultured starter, which gives the product a nutty, savoury flavour and causes it to solidify so that it can be cut into blocks. The beans remain visible under a velvety coating that resembles the rind you find on Brie. Their presence makes for a product that is firmer and more chewy than most other forms of tofu. In the wok, tempeh can be steamed, stir-fried, deep-fried or braised.

TVP/TEXTURED VEGETABLE PROTEIN

This meat substitute is made from soya flour from which the fat has been removed. It can be flavoured and shaped to mimic minced (ground) beef and is also sold in cubes or slices. The very low fat content means that it keeps well without refrigeration.

Above: Silken tofu.

Below: Tempeh.

SAUCES AND FLAVOURINGS

When you own a wok, being a spontaneous cook becomes second nature. It is fun to raid the pantry and refrigerator and rustle up a stir-fry. As long as you start with oil and aromatics, you can add almost any variety of vegetable, plus meat, poultry, tofu or whatever else takes your fancy. A good sauce, or a stock made from a paste, will bring all the flavours together.

CURRY PASTE BLOCKS

If you can find the imported curry pastes formed in blocks in specialist food stores, then do use them, as they impart a wonderful authentic flavour to the food. There are, however, also bottled curry sauces that make good substitutes. Shrimp paste has a very powerful flavour. It is made from salted, dried and pulverized shrimp, and is then compressed and sold in blocks or small cans or tubs. It must always be cooked, and used sparingly.

CHILLI SAUCE

Mainly used as a dipping sauce, this tastes great with crisp fried prawns (shrimp) or spiced noodle pancakes.

Below: There are several kinds of soy sauce from dark and thick to lighter, less rich types.

Above: Sweet chilli sauce.

It comes in various strengths and the sweetness also varies. The sweeter varieties go well with chicken.

FISH SAUCE

Read the list of ingredients for this Thai sauce, and you might be disinclined to try it. Opening the bottle could confirm your suspicions as it has a very pungent odour, but add it to a soup, stir-fry or braised dish and you will be amazed at the depth of flavour it imparts.

HOISIN SAUCE

Thick and sweet, this Chinese sauce is made from fermented beans, sugar, vinegar, salt, chillies, garlic and sesame oil, combined in varying proportions. It makes a good marinade, but you may need to thin it.

MISO PASTE

This Japanese fermented soy bean and grain paste is produced in various strengths. White miso is the lightest and sweetest. The most widely used form is the medium strength mugi miso, and there is also a very strong dark brown variety, hacho miso. Miso's principal use is for making different kinds of soup, but it can also be used in sauces, marinades and dressings.

OYSTER SAUCE

Popular in China and Thailand, this is based on soy sauce and oyster extract. It has a distinctive flavour and is great in soups and stir-fries.

PLUM SAUCE

Fruity, sweet and spicy, this is made from plums, ginger, garlic and chilli. It makes a good dip.

SOY SAUCE

Made from fermented soya beans, soy sauce is an essential ingredient throughout the Far East, and each country has its own version. There are three basic types, the colour governed by the stage at which the sauce is bottled, and the presence of other ingredients. The lightest soy sauce is Japanese. Then comes the Chinese light soy sauce. China also has a dark soy sauce that is good with red meats. Tamari is a Japanese dark sauce that is full of flavour but isn't too salty. Thailand has a sweet soy sauce.

TERIYAKI SAUCE

This Japanese sauce is sold commercially but you can make your own by mixing equal proportions of shoyu and mirin in a pan. Add a little sugar to sweeten the mixture. Stir over gentle heat until the sugar has dissolved, then cool. If not using immediately, store in the refrigerator.

Left: Dark hoisin sauce.

Ready-made Stir-fry Sauces

Dozens of different stir-fry sauces are on sale in the supermarket. The quality varies, but some are very good indeed, and are a boon when you've only got a few minutes to throw a meal together. Apart from the obvious sweet and sour, and black bean sauce, other examples include lemon and sesame seed, black bean with garlic, hoisin and spring onion (scallion) and spicy tomato Szechuan. Some sauces are more fusion food than authentic Asian, but why not? Owning a wok means opening your eyes to the wider possibilities it offers.

HERBS AND SPICES

Above: Kaffir lime leaves.

In view of the speed of wok cooking, any added flavourings need to deliver pretty smartly. Most herbs do the job well, but spices need to be chosen with care, as many of them have an impact only after lengthy cooking.

BASIL

Thai basil is a popular ingredient in South-east Asian cooking. It has a typical sweet basil aroma, overlaid with hints of aniseed or liquorice. The leaves are often added whole to stir-fries and curries. Another strain of basil, with a much more assertive flavour, is holy basil. This herb has a peppery taste, which only develops fully when heated. It is often used in soups and stir-fries, but isn't suitable for salads.

CORIANDER

Although you can use a wide range of herbs in wok cooking, coriander (cilantro) is probably the most useful. Its fresh green leaves have a distinctive, spicy flavour. Coriander roots and stems are often used in curry pastes.

Above: Shiso.

Add chopped coriander to stir-fries at the last minute or the flavour will be lost. Dried coriander is used in curry.

FIVE-SPICE POWDER

A classic spice mix widely used in Chinese cooking, particularly in braised dishes. It contains star anise, Szechuan peppercorns, fennel seeds, cloves and cinnamon and has a pungent, slightly sweet flavour.

KAFFIR LIME LEAVES

Although difficult to find fresh, lime leaves are easily obtained dried. They give a lovely authentic, warm, spicy citrus flavour to a dish.

MINT

Often used with fresh coriander in fillings for spring rolls and similar deep-fried snacks, mint is also good in a noodle salad.

PANDANUS LEAVES

These fragrant leaves are principally used as a wrapper, or as a liner for ramekins for poaching. The leaves look very attractive when wrapped around pieces of chicken, threaded on skewers and deep-fried in a hot wok.

SHISO

A herb with a distinctive aroma, this is an important ingredient in Japanese cooking. Despite being a form of mint, the flavour is redolent of basil.

STAR ANISE

This distinctive-looking spice has a warm flavour that puts it in the same category as cinnamon and nutmeg. It is used in savoury and sweet dishes.

Above: Star anise.

TAMARIND

Imagine a very intense lemon taste with no bitterness. That's tamarind, a popular product in South-east Asia. It is sold in blocks that need soaking, but can also be bought pre-prepared in jars.

Above: Pandanus leaves.

WASABI

This is often referred to as Japanese horseradish, even though it is no relation. Like watercress, it grows wild in mountain streams, but is also cultivated. Like mustard, it is mainly sold either as a paste or as a powder which must be mixed with warm water. Treat wasabi with caution – the pale green colour may look pretty but it packs a terrific punch, and too much could ruin a dish.

WINE FOR THE WOK

Rice wine seems to be far better suited to wok cooking than anything the grape can offer, and is used both as a marinade and in sauces. It is important to differentiate between sake, which is a dry rice wine used for drinking and cooking, and the much sweeter mirin, which is used only for cooking. These are Japanese products. The Chinese also make rice wine. Theirs tends to be dry, like sake, but with a distinctly different flavour. The best Chinese rice wine comes from Shaoxing, in eastern China. Mirin can be used as a marinade, often combined with soy sauce.

Right: Rice wine.

PREPARATION TECHNIQUES

Successful wok cooking is all about preparation, especially when you are stir-frying, which is so fast it is essential to have everything ready before you begin. That means slicing vegetables, meat or fish to the size required, having sauces handy and making sure that implements needed are within reach.

CUTTING AND SLICING VEGETABLES

Asian cooks take great care over the preparation of ingredients. There's an aesthetic reason for this – food must look as well as taste good – but careful cutting also serves a practical purpose. Cutting all the pieces to a similar size means they cook quickly and evenly.

Root Vegetables

Firm root vegetables, such as carrots, parsnips and mooli (daikon) can be diced, sliced or cut into matchsticks. Use a cook's knife or a cleaver. Trim the vegetable, then take a thin slice off each side to square it up. Slice lengthways. Pile the slices on top of each other and cut them into sticks.

Onions

Used for their flavour, all members of the onion family are used in stir-fries and other dishes. Shallots have a mild flavour but are fiddly to prepare. Spring onions (scallions) are often used cooked, raw and as a garnish in many Asian cooking traditions. They make a perfect stir-fry ingredient, as their flavour is retained. If shreds are called for, cut off the dark green top, then slice the portions of stem lengthways in half, then into strips.

Above: Use a mixture of peppers for maximum colour impact.

Above: Cut meat into small pieces or strips so that it cooks quickly.

Other Vegetables

Aubergines (eggplants), courgettes (zucchini), sweet (bell) peppers, green beans, mushrooms and corn are common stir-fry ingredients.

Less robust than root vegetables, courgettes shouldn't be cut too small. Ovals, sliced at an angle, work best. Aubergines are thinly sliced for tempura, cubed for slow-cooked dishes, or cut into strips for frying. If peppers

Below: Aubergine, sliced for tempura.

are called for in a dish, cut them in thin slices, as they can take longer to cook than other ingredients.

Mushrooms of all kinds are favourite ingredients. Shitake mushrooms are a particular favourite of Chinese and Thai cooks, and are often used dried for a more intense flavour.

If fresh corn is in season, and a recipe calls for it as an ingredient, use this instead of tinned or frozen. To free the corn from the cob, hold the top with one hand, and slice the kernels away.

Green beans for stir-fries should be the very freshest available; if they are slightly woody, trim the sides as well as the tops and bottoms, and slice thinly. Broccoli and cauliflower should be cut into small florets for stir-fries.

PREPARING MEAT, FISH AND POULTRY

How you prepare meat and fish depends on the type and dish, but for stir-fries you should always use the best and freshest cuts. The cheaper cuts, such as stewing beef or belly pork. are ideal for slow cooked dishes that have time to tenderize. When you are using chicken or pork in a stir-fry, you need to make sure it is cooked right through, and shows no sign of pinkness.

For stir-fries cut meat and fish across the grain. This not only helps the food to cook evenly, but also prevents it from disintegrating. Prawns (shrimp) and scallops can be left whole, and need only minutes to cook. They are usually the last ingredient to be added to a stir-fry, to prevent them going rubbery.

Below: Prawns can be left in their shells or peeled.

STIR-FRYING TECHNIQUES

Most of the cooking you are likely to do in your wok will be stir-frying, so it makes sense to get to grips with the technique from the start. Have all the ingredients close at hand, including measured items such as sauces.

PREHEATING THE WOK

The most important thing to remember is that the wok must be preheated. If the wok is hot when you add the oil, it will coat the surface with a thin film, preventing food from sticking. The best way to do this is to add a trickle of oil, necklace-fashion, around the inner rim so that it runs down evenly. You don't need much – 15–30ml/1–2 tbsp will be ample. Tilt the pan, if necessary, to spread the oil evenly.

Have the heat as high as possible if you are stir-frying meat, so that it is seared the moment it touches the wok. For fish or vegetables, the heat can be slightly lower. A simple test to ensure the wok is hot enough for stir-frying is to flick a few drops of water on to the surface after oiling. If this results in a loud sizzling sound, and the water immediately boils off, add your meat. If the water sizzles but remains visible for a few seconds before vanishing, the heat is right for fish or vegetables. Use oil with a high smoking point, such as groundnut (peanut) or corn oil.

COOKING AROMATICS

Individual recipes vary, but it is usual to start a stir-fry by adding aromatics such as garlic, ginger, chillies and spring onion (scallions) to the oil, then to fry meat, if used, and finish with the

Above: Sauces are added at the end of the cooking process.

vegetables. Cooking aromatics flavours the oil. If this is their only function, they are fished out before anything else is added to the wok.

STIR-FRYING MEAT

When stir-frying meat, don't overload the wok or you will bring down the temperature. Add a few pieces at a time, sear them for a few seconds, flip them over and sear the other side, then push them away from the centre, where the heat is concentrated, and add more meat to the well. When the meat has been sealed, either push the pieces on to the sloping sides of the wok, so they will stay warm without continuing to fry, or remove them to a dish.

STIR-FRYING VEGETABLES

Add the vegetables to the wok, starting with varieties that take the longest to cook, such as carrots, broccoli and

sweet (bell) peppers. Vegetables that need very little cooking, such as mooli (daikon) and mushrooms should be added next, with leafy vegetables tossed in right at the end. Keep the food on the move all the time, flipping and turning it with a spatula. Although the technique is called stir-frying, use a tossing and turning action, rather than stirring.

ADDING A SAUCE

When the vegetables are lightly cooked but still crisp, mix in the meat or other ingredients and then add any suggested sauces. A cornflour (cornstarch) mixture will thicken as well as flavour the mixture. If you are using a cornflour-based sauce, make a well in the stir-fry so you can stir it on its own for a minute or so before mixing it in.

Below: Make sure the oil in the wok is hot before adding any ingredients.

Below: When cooking aromatics, be careful not to let them burn.

Below: The wok is ideal for frying meat because of its high and even heat.

DEEP-FRYING TECHNIQUES

Provided a few safety precautions are taken, a wok is a useful pan for shallow and deep-frying. The shape means that you need less oil than in a conventional deep-fryer, yet still have a large surface area for cooking the food.

HEATING THE OIL

Start by making sure that the wok is stable. A flat-based wok is safest for deep-frying. If you use a round-based wok, make sure it will not wobble. Use a stand if necessary. The wok must be cold when the oil is added. This is the opposite advice to that given for stir-frying, when oil is added to a hot wok. Use an oil with a low smoking point and never fill the wok more than one-third full. This is more than adequate for most foods, and there will be less risk of the cook being splashed with hot fat or, worse, of the fat catching fire.

THE RIGHT TEMPERATURE

For deep-frying, oil needs to be at just the right temperature, so that the outside of the food becomes beautifully crisp while the centre cooks through to tender perfection. The precise temperature required will depend upon the density of what is being cooked and whether it has a coating of some kind, but around 180–190°C/350–375°F is suitable for most foods. A deep-fat thermometer, which can be clipped safely to the side of the wok before the oil is heated, is the safest and surest way of checking the temperature, but you can also test it by adding a cube of bread to the hot oil. The bread should brown in 45 seconds: if it sinks or fries

Below: Make sure there is enough oil for the volume of food being fried.

Above: Wrappers create a delicious crispy coating and keep food moist.

more slowly any food cooked in the wok would be greasy; if it burns, the same fate lies in wait for the food; if it sizzles on contact and bobs up to float on the surface, the temperature is just right.

COATING

Food can be coated in batter or a simple egg-and-breadcrumb mixture before being deep-fried. This protects, adds a contrasting texture and locks in the flavour. Dip the item to be coated in to the batter and gently shake off any excess before adding it to the hot oil. Flour or cornflour (cornstarch), egg and breadcrumbs can also be used for coating. Another method of protecting delicate food is to enclose it in a dough wrapper before deep-frying. This method is used for wontons and spring rolls, and the crispy result is delicious.

DEEP-FRYING TIPS

Don't overcrowd the wok. Add a few pieces at a time, lowering them gently into the oil to avoid splashing. Lift out carefully and either drain on a rack that

Above: Coating food before frying helps retain its moisture and flavour.

Hot Tips for Safe Deep-frying
- Don't fill the wok more than one-third full.
- Make sure it is stable.
- Be extra careful when adding food to the oil or retrieving it.
- Never leave a hot wok unattended.
- If the oil does catch fire, turn off the heat if you can and cover the wok with a heavy cloth or mat to exclude the air. This will put out the fire. Never throw water on an oil fire and don't try to move the wok.

has been clipped on to the side of the wok, or drain on kitchen paper and keep hot. Wait a minute or two before cooking successive batches, so that the oil gets the chance to return to its optimum temperature.

Below: Lift deep-fried food in and out of the hot wok with a long-handled tool.

STEAMING TECHNIQUES

This is a supremely healthy method, since the food is cooked without added fat and most of the nutrients are preserved. It is also simple, fast and efficient, whether you use a steamer specifically made for the wok or improvise with a trivet and a plate.

SUITABLE FOR STEAMING

All sorts of foods can be steamed, from fish to vegetables, poultry and even pancakes, custards and breads. Tender cuts of chicken cook well in the steamer but this is not the ideal cooking method for red meat. Check your chosen recipe for any advance preparation required. If you are cooking fish, is it whole or in portions? If whole, you may be advised to slit the skin and insert flavourings, such as fresh herbs, citrus slices or even a spicy rub. Delicate foods may need to be wrapped before being steamed. Banana leaves and lettuce leaves are popular for this purpose, as wraps or to line the steamer.

SELECTING A STEAMER

A steamer is simply a device for cooking foods by means of moist heat. The food should never touch the water that generates the steam, and the moisture must be trapped. You can steam food by simply placing it on a raised plate inside your wok, but steaming is simpler in a utensil designed for the purpose. Bamboo steamers are efficient and easy to use. So are stainless-steel steamers, but they are much more expensive. It is also possible to steam foods on the rack supplied with your wok, but this will only accommodate small amounts.

Below: Whole chickens, when steamed, have a special flavour and tenderness.

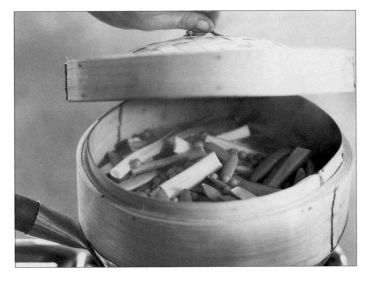

Above: A bamboo steamer is best when steaming in a wok, as it fits perfectly.

ASSEMBLING THE STEAMER

Food can be placed directly in the steamer basket, but this method tends to be reserved for dim sum or breads. It is more usual for a recipe to recommend lining the steamer with baking parchment or leaves before adding the food. This stops the food sticking and prevents small pieces from slipping through the slats. If you use this technique, make sure steam can still circulate. Using leaves for lining won't pose problems as steam will find its way around them, but parchment should be pierced. Alternatively, the food can be put on a plate or bowl inside the steamer so long as the steam holes are not blocked. Custards and some fish dishes are cooked this way.

Before you use a steamer in your wok for the first time, check the fit. You may have to use a trivet or upturned cup to keep the base of the steamer above the water. If a steamer is large, the sloping sides of the wok may prevent it from descending to the water level.

Steamer baskets are stackable, so you can cook several items at once, with the most delicate foods on top. The steamer will probably have its own cover, but if it doesn't, you will need to cover the wok itself, preferably with a domed lid so that condensed water runs down the sides and drips back into the water, rather than on to the food.

GETTING UP STEAM

The liquid to generate the steam can be water or stock. Aromatic flavourings like lemon grass, ginger or seaweed can be used to scent the steam. Fill the wok to a depth of around 5cm/2in, bring the liquid to the boil, carefully insert the steamer and cover with the lid. During steaming, keep checking the water level and top up if necessary. Angle the lid away from you to avoid being scalded.

Below: Individual fish custards are steamed to retain flavour and texture.

SIMMERING AND SMOKING

Although the wok is most closely associated with stir-fries and steamed food, it is also great for soups and sauced dishes such as Thai curries, braised pork belly or Beef Rendang. The frying stage that is the starting point for many of these dishes is easily accomplished in a wok, and after more ingredients are added, simmering is a cinch.

RAPID REDUCTION

The shape of the wok, with a wide surface area tapering to a narrow heat base, makes for rapid reduction of sauces. Where the aim is to concentrate the liquid, this is ideal, but you need to keep an eye on what's cooking, and top up the stock or sauce if necessary. For this reason, a wok isn't the best pan for a stew or similar dish that needs to be cooked for a very long time. A heavy pan is better for that purpose, but if you do use a wok, make it a stainless steel or non-stick one. Extended slow cooking in a carbon steel wok may erode the seasoned surface.

BLANCHING AND BOILING

For stir-frying, vegetables are usually cooked in relays, as some are much denser than others. Blanching toughies such as carrots and broccoli in boiling water gives them a head start so they can be stir-fried alongside more tender

Below: The wok is ideal for boiling or blanching green leafy vegetables.

Above: Fast boiling reduces a sauce, and gives a more intense flavour.

Above: Slow, gentle simmering produces a rich creamy taste and texture.

vegetables. Bring a wok of water to the boil, add the vegetables and cook for the required length of time (usually about 2–3 minutes). Lift the vegetables out of the wok with a skimmer or spider, plunge them into cold water so that they stop cooking, then drain and pat dry.

A wok can also be used for poaching fruit and cooking rice or noodles.

Wok Smoking

You don't need elaborate equipment to smoke poultry or seafood. A carbon steel wok works well, especially if you follow the Chinese tradition and use a tea leaf mixture as the smoking medium. The only drawback is the obvious one – use an extractor fan or be prepared for your smoke alarm to go off.

1 Line a carbon steel wok (not any other type) with foil, allowing a generous overlap. Sprinkle in 30ml/2 tbsp each of raw long grain rice, sugar and tea leaves.

2 Fit a wire rack on top of the wok and place the food to be smoked in a single layer on top. Mackerel fillets, salmon and duck or chicken breast portions work well. Cover the wok with a lid or inverted pan and cook over a very high heat until you see smoke.

3 Lower the heat so that the smoke reduces to wisps that seep from under the lid, and cook until the food is done. A mackerel fillet takes around 8–10 minutes; large fresh prawns (shrimp) 5–7 minutes, duck or chicken breast portions 18–20 minutes.

COOKING RICE AND NOODLES

Many of the Chinese and Thai recipes in this book are based on rice or noodles, which may be used as an accompaniment rather than part of the main dish. If you are using your wok for the meat or vegetable accompaniment, you will probably be cooking your rice or noodles in a pan.

COOKING RICE

There are several ways of cooking rice, but the absorption method is best for jasmine rice, basmati, short grain rice and glutinous rice. The proportion of water to rice will depend on the type of rice used, but as a guide, you will need about 600ml/1 pint/2½ cups water for every 225g/8oz/generous 1 cup rice.

1 Rinse the rice thoroughly and put it in a pan. Pour in the water. Do not add salt. Bring to the boil, then reduce the heat to the lowest possible setting.

2 Cover tightly and cook for 20–25 minutes, or until the liquid is absorbed.

3 Without lifting the lid, remove the pan from the heat. Leave it to stand in a warm place for 5 minutes to rest, and complete the cooking process. If cooked rice is required for a fried rice dish, cool it quickly, then chill it before frying.

Steamed Sticky Rice

Thais like their accompanying rice to be sticky. To get the authentic texture steam it in a bamboo steamer. Make sure you buy the right rice, usually called sticky or glutinous rice.

Rinse the rice in several changes of water, then leave to soak overnight in a bowl of cold water. Line a large bamboo steamer with muslin (cheesecloth). Drain the rice and spread out evenly on the muslin. Cover the rice and steam for 25–30 minutes, until the rice is tender. (Check the water level and add more if necessary.)

Making a Risotto in the Wok

The wok is not only suitable for Asian dishes, it also makes great risotto. Have the hot stock ready in a pan.

Melt butter, oil or a mixture in a wok and fry an onion. Add risotto rice and stir to coat the grains. Add a dash of white wine, then when that is absorbed begin adding hot stock, a ladleful at a time. Stir constantly until the stock is absorbed, then add more. It will take about 20 minutes for the rice to become tender. Add a little butter and stir in. Remove the pan from the heat and cover. Leave for 2 minutes, then serve.

COOKING NOODLES

If you are cooking noodles, either to serve solo or as part of a composite dish, do not rely entirely on the recipe – check the packet, too. Par-cooked noodles only need to be soaked in hot water; others must be boiled. Ready-to-use noodles need no attention at all, and can simply be added to a stir-fry and tossed over the heat until hot.

Preparing Rice Noodles
Rice noodles have been par-cooked when you buy them, so they only need to be soaked in hot water before use.

Add the noodles to a large bowl of just-boiled water and leave for 5–10 minutes or until softened, stirring occasionally to separate.

Preparing Wheat Noodles
Wheat noodles have to be cooked in boiling water. They take very little time, however.

Bring a large pan of water to the boil, add the fresh egg noodles and cook for 2–4 minutes or until tender. Drain well. If the noodles are going to be mixed into a stir-fry and cooked further, give them just 2 minutes initially.

DIPS AND GARNISHES

With a wok, it takes next to no time to rustle up treats like spring rolls, potato puffs and crisp-fried crab claws. Try them with these delicious dips.

Thai Red Curry Dip

This tastes good with mini spring rolls, or can be tossed with rice noodles for a simple accompaniment.

SERVES 4

  200ml/7fl oz/scant 1 cup coconut cream
  10–15ml/2–3 tsp Thai red curry paste
  4 spring onions (scallions), plus extra, thinly sliced, to garnish
  30ml/2 tbsp chopped fresh coriander (cilantro)
  1 fresh red chilli, seeded and thinly sliced in rings
  5ml/1 tsp soy sauce
  juice of 1 lime
  sugar, to taste
  25g/1oz/3 tbsp dry-roasted peanuts, finely chopped
  salt and ground black pepper

Pour the coconut cream into a small bowl and stir in the curry paste. Trim the spring onions, slice them diagonally, then stir into the coconut cream with the coriander, chilli, soy sauce and lime juice. Add enough sugar to give a sweet-sour flavour and season with salt and pepper. Spoon into a serving bowl and top with the peanuts and thinly sliced spring onion.

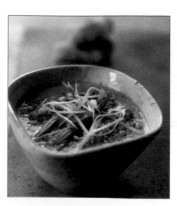

Wasabi and Soy Dip

Try this with crab cakes or fish cakes. The combination works extremely well, especially if you add a squeeze of lime just before dipping.

SERVES 4

  175ml/6fl oz/¾ cup soy sauce or shoyu
  10ml/2 tsp wasabi paste
  2 spring onions (scallions), diagonally sliced
  1 fresh red chilli, seeded and thinly sliced in rings (optional)

Mix the soy sauce or shoyu with the wasabi paste in a bowl. Float the spring onion slices on top. The chilli slices can be added or left out, depending on how spicy you want the dip to be. Top with just one or two rings for colour.

Sweet Chilli Sauce

This sweet, spicy sauce has a wonderfully aromatic flavour and lovely translucent red colour. It can be used both for flavouring and as a dipping sauce. Any remaining sauce can be stored in the refrigerator in an airtight container for 1–2 weeks.

SERVES 4

  6 large red chillies
  60ml/4 tbsp white vinegar
  250g/9oz caster (superfine) sugar
  5ml/1 tsp salt
  4 garlic cloves, chopped

Place the chillies in a food processor. Add the vinegar, sugar, salt and garlic. Blend until smooth, transfer to a pan and cook over a medium heat until thickened. Leave to cool and then transfer to a bowl.

GREAT GARNISHES

Thai cooks enjoy garnishing their dishes with beautifully cut vegetables. Here are some suggestions for easy finishing touches that look fabulous.

Tamarind Sauce

This sweet, tangy dipping sauce has a fruity flavour and is perfect served with spicy deep-fried snacks. The quantities here are suitable for one serving, but if there is any left over, transfer to an airtight container and store in the refrigerator for 1–2 weeks.

MAKES 1 SMALL JAR

90ml/6 tbsp tamarind paste
90ml/6 tbsp water
45ml/3 tbsp caster (superfine) sugar

Place all the ingredients in a small pan and bring the mixture to the boil. Reduce the heat and cook gently for 3–4 minutes, stirring occasionally. Remove the pan from the heat and transfer to a small bowl. Leave to cool before serving.

Ginger and Hoisin Dip

Chunky and bursting with flavour, this dip is delicious with prawn (shrimp) crackers. The dip can be stored in the refrigerator for up to 1 week.

SERVES 4

60ml/4 tbsp hoisin sauce
120ml/4fl oz/$\frac{1}{2}$ cup passata (bottled strained tomatoes)
4 spring onions (scallions), thinly sliced
4cm/1$\frac{1}{2}$in piece fresh root ginger, peeled and finely chopped
2 fresh red chillies, seeded and cut into fine strips
2 garlic cloves, crushed
few drops of roasted sesame oil

Mix the hoisin and passata in a bowl. Stir in the spring onions, ginger, chillies and crushed garlic. Add the sesame oil, mix well and serve.

A cucumber frill makes a lovely garnish for duck, steamed salmon, a stir-fry or salad. Cut a cucumber in half lengthways. Scoop out the seeds from one half and place it cut side down. Using a knife held at an angle, thinly slice the cucumber, cutting almost through so the slices remain attached at the base. Fan the slices out. Turn in alternate slices to form loops, then bend into a semi-circle with the loops on the outside, so that they resemble petals.

1 Using a small pair of scissors or a slim-bladed knife, slit a fresh red chilli carefully lengthways from the tip to within 1cm/$\frac{1}{2}$in of the stem end. Repeat this at regular intervals around the chilli, keeping the stem end intact, until it resembles a tassel. Slit more chillies in the same way.

2 Rinse the chillies in cold water to wash away the seeds. Place in a bowl of iced water and chill for at least 4 hours. For very curly chilli flowers, leave the bowl in the refrigerator overnight.

Wasabi paste

This bright green paste packs a whopping punch. It is made from a Japanese herb and tastes like a cross between hot mustard and horseradish. A little goes a long way to flavour dips and sauces. Try mixing it with mayonnaise for a delicious dip to serve with steamed asparagus. The most convenient way to buy wasabi is in a tube. If you use powdered wasabi, mix it in an egg cup with the same volume of tepid water, then stand the egg cup upside down for 10 minutes to allow the flavour to develop without letting the wasabi dry out.

CRISPY FINGER FOOD AND APPETIZERS

A wok isn't just for wonderful main courses — it is a great accessory when it comes to the little treats that add spice to life. Spring rolls, samosas and puff pastry parcels can be cooked to crisp perfection in minutes, ready for dipping into scrumptious sauces. Spiced Noodle Pancakes and Pea and Potato Pakoras provide two more good reasons for heating the oil and starting to sizzle. For serving with drinks, try Roasted Coconut Cashew Nuts — piled in paper cones to save fingers from getting sticky — or choose one of the more substantial snacks that can double as an appetizer.

PRAWN AND SESAME TOASTS

THESE ATTRACTIVE LITTLE TOAST TRIANGLES ARE IDEAL FOR SERVING WITH PRE-DINNER DRINKS AND ARE ALWAYS A FAVOURITE HOT SNACK AT PARTIES. THEY ARE SURPRISINGLY EASY TO PREPARE AND YOU CAN COOK THEM IN YOUR WOK FOR JUST A FEW MINUTES. SERVE THEM WITH A SWEET CHILLI SAUCE.

SERVES FOUR

INGREDIENTS
    225g/8oz peeled raw prawns (shrimp)
    15ml/1 tbsp sherry
    15ml/1 tbsp soy sauce
    30ml/2 tbsp cornflour (cornstarch)
    2 egg whites
    4 slices white bread
    115g/4oz/½ cup sesame seeds
    oil, for deep-frying
    sweet chilli sauce,
        to serve

1 Process the prawns, sherry, soy sauce and cornflour in a food processor.

2 In a grease-free bowl, whisk the egg whites until stiff. Fold them into the prawn and cornflour mixture.

3 Cut each slice of bread into four triangular quarters. Spread out the sesame seeds on a large plate. Spread the prawn paste over one side of each bread triangle, then press the coated sides into the sesame seeds so that they stick and cover the prawn paste.

4 Heat the oil in a wok or deep-fryer, to 190°C/375°F or until a cube of bread, added to the oil, browns in about 45 seconds. Add the toasts, a few at a time, prawn side down, and deep-fry for 2–3 minutes, then turn and fry on the other side until golden.

5 Drain on kitchen paper and serve hot with sweet chilli sauce.

Energy 392Kcal/1634kJ; Protein 19.1g; Carbohydrate 21.1g, of which sugars 1.2g; Fat 25.8g, of which saturates 3.4g; Cholesterol 110mg; Calcium 270mg; Fibre 2.7g; Sodium 557mg.

ROASTED COCONUT CASHEW NUTS

SERVE THESE WOK-FRIED HOT AND SWEET CASHEW NUTS IN PAPER OR CELLOPHANE CONES AT PARTIES. NOT ONLY DO THEY LOOK ENTICING AND TASTE TERRIFIC, BUT THE CONES HELP TO KEEP CLOTHES AND HANDS CLEAN AND CAN SIMPLY BE CRUMPLED UP AND THROWN AWAY AFTERWARDS.

SERVES SIX TO EIGHT

INGREDIENTS
    15ml/1 tbsp groundnut (peanut) oil
    30ml/2 tbsp clear honey
    250g/9oz/2 cups cashew nuts
    115g/4oz/1⅓ cups desiccated (dry
        unsweetened shredded) coconut
    2 small fresh red chillies, seeded and
        finely chopped
    salt and ground black pepper

VARIATIONS
Almonds also work well, or choose
peanuts for a more economical snack.

1 Heat the oil in a wok or large frying
pan and then stir in the honey. After a
few seconds add the nuts and coconut
and stir-fry until both are golden brown.

2 Add the chillies, with salt and pepper
to taste. Toss until all the ingredients
are well mixed. Serve warm or cooled in
paper cones or on saucers.

Energy 301Kcal/1247kJ; Protein 7.2g; Carbohydrate 9.7g, of which sugars 5.5g; Fat 26.2g, of which saturates 11.1g; Cholesterol 0mg; Calcium 14mg; Fibre 3g; Sodium 95mg.

GOLDEN BEEF AND POTATO PUFFS

THESE CRISP, GOLDEN PILLOWS OF PASTRY FILLED WITH SPICED BEEF AND POTATOES ARE DELICIOUS SERVED PIPING HOT, STRAIGHT FROM THE WOK. THE LIGHT, FLAKY PASTRY PUFFS UP WONDERFULLY IN THE HOT OIL AND CONTRASTS ENTICINGLY WITH THE FRAGRANT SPICED BEEF FILLING WITHIN.

SERVES FOUR

INGREDIENTS

15ml/1 tbsp sunflower oil
½ small onion, finely chopped
3 garlic cloves, crushed
5ml/1 tsp finely grated fresh root ginger
1 fresh red chilli, seeded and finely chopped
30ml/2 tbsp hot curry powder
75g/3oz minced (ground) beef
115g/4oz mashed potato
60ml/4 tbsp chopped fresh coriander (cilantro)
2 sheets ready-rolled, fresh puff pastry
1 egg, lightly beaten
vegetable oil, for frying
salt and ground black pepper
fresh coriander leaves, to garnish
tomato ketchup, to serve

1 Heat the oil in a wok, then add the onion, garlic, ginger and chilli. Stir-fry over a medium heat for 2–3 minutes. Add the curry powder and beef and stir-fry over a high heat for a further 4–5 minutes, or until the beef is browned and just cooked through, then remove from the heat.

2 Transfer the beef mixture to a large bowl and add the mashed potato and chopped fresh coriander. Stir well, then season and set aside.

COOK'S TIP
For a change in texture, you can use ready-made shortcrust pastry in place of the puff pastry. The puffs will be transformed into little golden crescents that have a firmer, crisper shell but the same succulent beef filling.

3 Lay the pastry sheets on a clean, dry surface and cut out 8 rounds, using a 7.5cm/3in pastry (cookie) cutter.

4 Place a large spoonful of the beef mixture in the centre of each pastry round. Brush the edges of the pastry with the beaten egg and fold each round in half to enclose the filling. Press and crimp the edges with the tines of a fork to seal.

5 Fill a wok one-third full of oil and heat to 180ºC/350ºF or until a cube of bread, dropped into the oil, browns in 40 seconds.

6 Deep-fry the puffs, in batches, for 2–3 minutes until puffed up and golden brown. Drain on kitchen paper and serve garnished with fresh coriander leaves. Offer a small bowl of tomato ketchup for dipping.

VARIATION
Try equal quantities of tomato ketchup and brown sauce as an alternative dip.

Energy 408Kcal/1695kJ; Protein 9g; Carbohydrate 24.2g, of which sugars 1.8g; Fat 31.8g, of which saturates 4.2g; Cholesterol 67mg; Calcium 46mg; Fibre 0.5g; Sodium 202mg.

TUNG TONG

*POPULARLY CALLED "GOLD BAGS", THESE CRISP PASTRY PURSES HAVE A CORIANDER-FLAVOURED
FILLING BASED ON WATER CHESTNUTS AND CORN. THEY ARE THE PERFECT VEGETARIAN SNACK, CRISP
AND CRUNCHY ON THE OUTSIDE, WITH A SUCCULENT CORN AND WATER CHESTNUT FILLING.*

MAKES EIGHTEEN

INGREDIENTS
  18 spring roll wrappers, about
    8cm/3¼in square, thawed
    if frozen
  oil, for deep-frying
  plum sauce, to serve
For the filling
  4 baby corn cobs
  130g/4½oz can water chestnuts,
    drained and chopped
  1 shallot, coarsely chopped
  1 egg, separated
  30ml/2 tbsp cornflour (cornstarch)
  60ml/4 tbsp water
  small bunch fresh coriander
    (cilantro), chopped
  salt and ground black pepper

1 Make the filling. Place the baby corn, water chestnuts, shallot and egg yolk in a food processor or blender. Process to a coarse paste. Place the egg white in a cup and whisk it lightly with a fork.

2 Put the cornflour in a small pan and stir in the water until smooth. Add the corn mixture and chopped coriander and season with salt and pepper to taste. Cook over a low heat, stirring constantly, until thickened.

3 Leave the filling to cool slightly, then place 5ml/1 tsp in the centre of a spring roll wrapper. Brush the edges with the beaten egg white, then gather up the points and press them firmly together to make a pouch or bag.

4 Repeat with the remaining wrappers and filling. Heat the oil in a wok to 190°C/375°F or until a cube of bread, added to the oil, browns in about 45 seconds. Fry the bags, in batches, for about 5 minutes, until golden brown. Drain on kitchen paper and serve hot, with the plum sauce.

Energy 55Kcal/229kJ; Protein 1.2g; Carbohydrate 6.3g, of which sugars 0.4g; Fat 2.9g, of which saturates 0.4g; Cholesterol 12mg; Calcium 19mg; Fibre 0.5g; Sodium 42mg.

FIRECRACKERS

IT'S EASY TO SEE HOW THESE PASTRY-WRAPPED PRAWN SNACKS GOT THEIR NAME. NOT ONLY DO THEY WHIZ AROUND IN THE WOK LIKE ROCKETS, BUT WHEN YOU BITE INTO THEM THEIR CONTENTS EXPLODE WITH FLAVOUR. MARINATING THE PRAWNS IN CURRY PASTE MAKES ALL THE DIFFERENCE.

3 Place a wonton wrapper on the work surface at an angle so that it forms a diamond shape, then fold the top corner over so that the point is in the centre. Place a prawn, slits down, on the wrapper, with the tail projecting from the folded end, then fold the bottom corner over the other end of the prawn.

4 Fold each side of the wrapper over in turn to make a tightly folded roll. Tie a noodle in a bow around the roll and set it aside. Repeat with the remaining prawns and wrappers.

5 Heat the oil in a wok to 190°C/375°F or until a cube of bread, added to the oil, browns in 40 seconds. Fry the prawns, a few at a time, for 5–8 minutes, until golden brown and cooked through. Drain well on kitchen paper and keep hot while you cook the remaining batches.

COOK'S TIP

Soak the egg noodles to be used as ties for the rolls in a bowl of boiling water for 2–3 minutes, until soft, drain, refresh under cold running water and drain.

MAKES SIXTEEN

INGREDIENTS
  16 large, raw king prawns (jumbo
    shrimp), heads and shells removed
    but tails left on
  5ml/1 tsp red curry paste
  15ml/1 tbsp Thai fish sauce
  16 small wonton wrappers, about
    8cm/3¼ in square, thawed if frozen
  16 fine egg noodles, soaked
    (see Cook's Tip)
  oil, for deep-frying

1 Place the prawns on their sides and cut two slits through the underbelly of each, one about 1cm/½ in from the head end and the other about 1cm/½ in from the first cut, cutting across the prawn. This will prevent the prawns from curling when they are cooked.

2 Mix the curry paste with the fish sauce in a shallow dish. Add the prawns and turn them in the mixture until they are well coated. Cover and leave to marinate for 10 minutes.

Energy 71Kcal/298kJ; Protein 3.2g; Carbohydrate 7.1g, of which sugars 0.2g; Fat 3.5g, of which saturates 0.5g; Cholesterol 25mg; Calcium 20mg; Fibre 0.3g; Sodium 30mg.

CRISP-FRIED JAPANESE PANKO PRAWNS

WHEN BUTTERFLIED AND BATTERED TIGER PRAWNS ARE DEEP-FRIED IN THE WOK, THEY CURL UP BEAUTIFULLY, AND LOOK GORGEOUS ON DARK GREEN SEAWEED TOPPED WITH WHITE RICE. WASABI, SOY SAUCE, SWEET CHILLI SAUCE AND PICKLED GINGER ARE TRADITIONAL ACCOMPANIMENTS.

SERVES FOUR

INGREDIENTS

   20 large raw tiger or king prawns
     (jumbo shrimp), heads removed
   30ml/2 tbsp cornflour (cornstarch)
   3 large (US extra large) eggs,
     lightly beaten
   150g/5oz *panko* (Japanese-style
     breadcrumbs)
   sunflower oil, for frying
   4 sheets of nori
   400g/14oz cooked sushi rice
   wasabi, soy sauce, sweet chilli sauce
     and pickled ginger, to serve

1 Peel and devein the prawns, leaving the tails on. Using a small, sharp knife, cut down the back of each prawn, without cutting all the way through, and gently press the prawns out flat to butterfly them.

2 Place the cornflour, beaten eggs and *panko* in 3 separate bowls. Dip each prawn first in the cornflour mixture, next in the egg and then in the *panko,* to coat evenly. Fill a wok one-third full of sunflower oil and heat to 180°C/350°F (or until a cube of bread, added to the oil, browns in 45 seconds).

3 Working in batches, deep-fry the prawns for 1 minute, or until lightly golden and crisp. Remove with a slotted spoon and drain on kitchen paper.

4 Carefully cut each nori sheet into a 10cm/4in square. Place each square on a serving plate and divide the sushi rice among them, then spread out the rice using the back of a spoon. Top each serving with 5 deep-fried prawns and serve with wasabi, soy sauce, sweet chilli sauce and pickled ginger.

COOK'S TIP
Panko are Japanese-style breadcrumbs, which give a fabulously crunchy result when deep-fried. They make the perfect coating for these tender, juicy prawns, which remain unbelievably succulent when cooked. If you can't find panko, use coarse, dried breadcrumbs instead.

Energy 472Kcal/1989kJ; Protein 20.2g; Carbohydrate 63g, of which sugars 1g; Fat 17.4g, of which saturates 2.8g; Cholesterol 240mg; Calcium 127mg; Fibre 0.9g; Sodium 437mg.

CRISP-FRIED CRAB CLAWS

CRAB CLAWS ARE READILY AVAILABLE FROM THE FREEZER CABINET OF MANY ASIAN STORES AND SUPERMARKETS. THAW THEM THOROUGHLY AND DRY ON KITCHEN PAPER BEFORE COATING THEM.

SERVES FOUR

INGREDIENTS
50g/2oz/⅓ cup rice flour
15ml/1 tbsp cornflour (cornstarch)
2.5ml/½ tsp granulated sugar
1 egg
60ml/4 tbsp cold water
1 lemon grass stalk
2 garlic cloves, finely chopped
15ml/1 tbsp chopped fresh
  coriander (cilantro)
1–2 fresh red chillies, seeded and
  finely chopped
5ml/1 tsp Thai fish sauce
vegetable oil, for deep-frying
12 half-shelled crab claws, thawed
  if frozen
ground black pepper
For the chilli vinegar dip
45ml/3 tbsp granulated sugar
120ml/4fl oz/½ cup water
120ml/4fl oz/½ cup red
  wine vinegar
15ml/1 tbsp Thai fish sauce
2–4 fresh red chillies, seeded
  and chopped

1 First make the chilli vinegar dip. Mix the sugar and water in a pan. Heat gently, stirring until the sugar has dissolved, then bring to the boil. Lower the heat and simmer for 5–7 minutes. Stir in the rest of the ingredients, pour into a serving bowl and set aside.

2 Combine the rice flour, cornflour and sugar in a bowl. Beat the egg with the cold water, then stir the egg and water mixture into the flour mixture and beat well until it forms a light batter.

3 Cut off the lower 5cm/2in of the lemon grass stalk and chop it finely. Add the lemon grass to the batter, with the garlic, coriander, red chillies and fish sauce. Stir in pepper to taste.

4 Heat the oil in a wok or deep-fryer to 190°C/375°F or until a cube of bread browns in 40 seconds. Dip the crab claws into the batter, then fry, in batches, until golden. Serve with the dip.

Energy 222Kcal/926kJ; Protein 10.1g; Carbohydrate 16.9g, of which sugars 0g; Fat 12.8g, of which saturates 1.7g; Cholesterol 78mg; Calcium 62mg; Fibre 0.3g; Sodium 256mg.

DEEP-FRIED SMALL PRAWNS AND CORN

INSPIRED BY THE JAPANESE DISH CALLED TEMPURA, THIS SIMPLE SNACK FOOD IS A GOOD WAY OF USING UP SMALL QUANTITIES OF VEGETABLES AND PRAWNS. IT IS EASY TO COOK IN A WOK.

SERVES FOUR

INGREDIENTS
   200g/7oz small cooked, peeled
      prawns (shrimp)
   4–5 button (white) mushrooms
   4 spring onions (scallions)
   75g/3oz/½ cup canned, drained or
      frozen sweetcorn, thawed
   30ml/2 tbsp frozen peas, thawed
   vegetable oil, for deep-frying
   chives, to garnish
For the tempura batter
   300ml/½ pint/1¼ cups ice-cold water
   2 eggs, beaten
   150g/5oz/1¼ cups plain
      (all-purpose) flour
   1.5ml/¼ tsp baking powder
For the dipping sauce
   400ml/14fl oz/1⅔ cups second dashi
      stock, made with instant dashi
      powder and water
   100ml/3fl oz/scant ½ cup shoyu
   100ml/3fl oz/scant ½ cup mirin
   15ml/1 tbsp chopped chives

1 Roughly chop half the prawns. Cut the mushrooms into small cubes. Slice the white part from the spring onions and chop this roughly.

2 To make the tempura batter, in a medium mixing bowl, mix the cold water and eggs. Add the flour and baking powder, and very roughly fold in with a pair of chopsticks or a fork. Do not beat. The batter should still be quite lumpy. Heat plenty of oil in a wok to 170°C/338°F.

3 Mix the prawns and vegetables into the batter. Pour a quarter of the batter into a small bowl, then drop gently into the oil. Using wooden spoons, carefully gather the scattered batter to form a fist-size ball. Deep-fry until golden. Drain on kitchen paper.

4 In a small pan, mix all the liquid dipping-sauce ingredients together and bring to the boil, then immediately turn off the heat. Sprinkle with chives.

5 Garnish the fritters with chives, and serve with the dipping sauce.

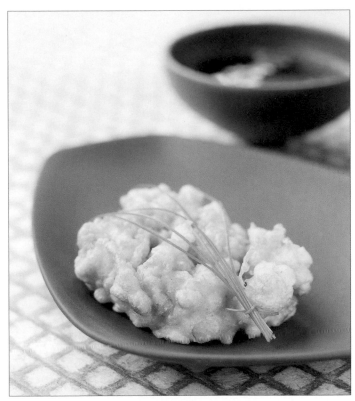

Energy 246Kcal/1039kJ; Protein 17.6g; Carbohydrate 37.4g, of which sugars 4.7g; Fat 4g, of which saturates 1g; Cholesterol 193mg; Calcium 117mg; Fibre 2g; Sodium 1963mg.

DEEP-FRIED LAYERED SHIITAKE AND SCALLOPS

A WOK DOES DOUBLE DUTY FOR MAKING THESE MUSHROOM AND SEAFOOD TREATS. THE NAGA-IMO (A TYPE OF YAM) IS STEAMED IN A BAMBOO BASKET, AND LATER THE WOK IS USED FOR DEEP-FRYING. THE SNACKS ARE DELICATE; USE A KNIFE AND FORK IF CHOPSTICKS PROVE TRICKY.

SERVES FOUR

INGREDIENTS
4 scallops
8 large fresh shiitake mushrooms
225g/8oz naga-imo, unpeeled
20ml/4 tsp miso
50g/2oz/1 cup fresh breadcrumbs
cornflour (cornstarch), for dusting
vegetable oil, for deep-frying
2 eggs, beaten
salt
4 lemon wedges, to serve

4 Wait until the naga-imo is cool enough to handle. Skin, then mash the flesh in a bowl with a masher, getting rid of any lumps. Add the miso and mix well. Take the breadcrumbs into your hands and break them down finely. Mix half into the mashed naga-imo, keeping the rest on a small plate.

7 Spread another 5ml/1 tsp mashed naga-imo on to the scallop and shape to completely cover. Make sure all the ingredients are clinging together. Repeat to make eight little mounds.

8 Heat the oil to 150°C/300°F. Place the beaten eggs in a shallow container. Dust the shiitake and scallop mounds with cornflour, then dip into the egg. Handle with care as the mash and scallop are quite soft. Coat well with the remaining breadcrumbs and deep-fry in the oil until golden. Drain well on kitchen paper. Serve hot on individual plates with a wedge of lemon.

1 Slice the scallops in two horizontally, then sprinkle with salt. Remove the stalks from the shiitake by cutting them off with a knife. Discard the stalks.

2 Cut shallow slits on the top of the shiitake to form a "hash" symbol or cut slits to form a white cross. Sprinkle with a little salt.

3 Heat a steamer and steam the naga-imo for 10–15 minutes, or until soft. Test with a skewer. Leave to cool.

5 Fill the underneath of the shiitake caps with a scoop of mashed naga-imo. Smooth down with the flat edge of a knife and dust the mash with cornflour.

6 Add a little mash to a slice of scallop and place on top.

VARIATION
For a vegetarian option, use 16 shiitake mushrooms. Sandwich the naga-imo mash between two shiitake to make 8 bundles. Deep-fry in the same way as the scallop version.

COOK'S TIPS
• Fresh naga-imo produces a slimy liquid when it's cut. Try not to touch this as some people may react and develop a mild rash. When it's cooked, it is perfectly safe to touch.
• If you can't find naga-imo, use yam or 115g/4oz each of potatoes and peeled Jerusalem artichokes instead. Steam the potatoes and boil the artichokes until both are tender.

Energy 247Kcal/1032kJ; Protein 14.1g; Carbohydrate 15.5g, of which sugars 4.5g; Fat 14.8g, of which saturates 2.3g; Cholesterol 113mg; Calcium 57mg; Fibre 1.9g; Sodium 213mg.

CRISPY SALT AND PEPPER SQUID

THESE DELICIOUS MORSELS OF SQUID LOOK STUNNING AND ARE PERFECT SERVED WITH DRINKS, OR AS AN APPETIZER. THE CRISP, GOLDEN COATING CONTRASTS BEAUTIFULLY WITH THE SUCCULENT SQUID INSIDE. SERVE THEM PIPING HOT STRAIGHT FROM THE WOK.

SERVES FOUR

INGREDIENTS
    750g/1lb 10oz fresh squid, cleaned
    juice of 4–5 lemons
    15ml/1 tbsp freshly ground
      black pepper
    15ml/1 tbsp sea salt
    10ml/2 tsp caster (superfine) sugar
    115g/4oz/1 cup cornflour
      (cornstarch)
    3 egg whites, lightly beaten
    vegetable oil, for deep-frying
    chilli sauce or sweet-and-sour sauce,
      for dipping
    skewers, to serve

1 Cut the squid into large bitesize pieces and score a diamond pattern on each piece, using a sharp knife or a cleaver.

2 Trim the tentacles. Place in a large mixing bowl and pour over the lemon juice. Cover and marinate for 10–15 minutes. Drain well and pat dry.

3 In a separate bowl mix together the pepper, salt, sugar and cornflour. Dip the squid pieces in the egg whites and then toss lightly in the seasoned flour, shaking off any excess.

4 Fill a wok one-third full of oil and heat to 180°C/350°F or until a cube of bread, dropped into the oil, browns in 40 seconds. Working in batches, deep-fry the squid for 1 minute. Drain on kitchen paper and serve threaded on to skewers with chilli or sweet-and-sour sauce.

COOK'S TIP
Keep egg whites in the freezer, ready to thaw for use in dishes such as this.

Energy 346Kcal/1462kJ; Protein 31.2g; Carbohydrate 31.3g, of which sugars 2.6g; Fat 11.6g, of which saturates 1.8g; Cholesterol 422mg; Calcium 32mg; Fibre 0g; Sodium 1741mg.

SPICED NOODLE PANCAKES

THE DELICATE RICE NOODLES PUFF UP IN THE HOT OIL TO GIVE A FABULOUS CRUNCHY BITE THAT MELTS IN THE MOUTH. FOR MAXIMUM ENJOYMENT, SERVE THE GOLDEN PANCAKES AS SOON AS THEY ARE COOKED AND SAVOUR THE SUBTLE BLEND OF SPICES AND WONDERFULLY CRISP TEXTURE.

SERVES FOUR

INGREDIENTS
150g/5oz dried thin rice noodles
1 fresh red chilli, finely diced
10ml/2 tsp garlic salt
5ml/1 tsp ground ginger
¼ small red onion, very finely diced
5ml/1 tsp finely chopped lemon grass
5ml/1 tsp ground cumin
5ml/1 tsp ground coriander
large pinch of ground turmeric
salt
vegetable oil, for frying
sweet chilli sauce, for dipping

1 Roughly break up the noodles and place in a large bowl. Pour over enough boiling water to cover, and soak for 4–5 minutes. Drain and rinse under cold water. Dry on kitchen paper.

2 Transfer the noodles to a bowl and add the chilli, garlic salt, ground ginger, red onion, lemon grass, ground cumin, coriander and turmeric. Toss well to mix, and season with salt.

COOK'S TIP
For deep-frying, choose very thin rice noodles. These can be cooked dry, but here are soaked and seasoned first.

3 Heat 5–6cm/2–2½in oil in a wok. Working in batches, drop tablespoons of the noodle mixture into the oil. Flatten using the back of a skimmer and cook for 1–2 minutes on each side until crisp and golden. Lift out from the wok.

4 Drain the noodle pancakes on kitchen paper and serve immediately with the chilli sauce for dipping.

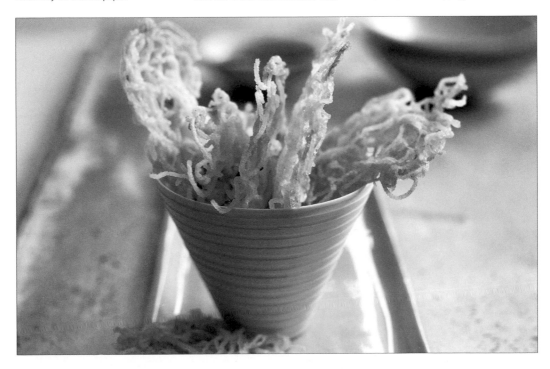

Energy 190Kcal/791kJ; Protein 2g; Carbohydrate 31.8g, of which sugars 0.9g; Fat 5.6g, of which saturates 0.7g; Cholesterol 0mg; Calcium 9mg; Fibre 0.2g; Sodium 496mg.

THAI SPRING ROLLS

CRUNCHY SPRING ROLLS ARE AS POPULAR IN THAILAND AS THEY ARE IN CHINA. THAIS FILL THEIR
VERSION WITH A DELICIOUS GARLIC, PORK AND NOODLE MIXTURE.

MAKES TWENTY-FOUR

INGREDIENTS
    24 x 15cm/6in square spring roll
        wrappers, thawed if frozen
    30ml/2 tbsp plain (all-purpose) flour
    vegetable oil, for deep-frying
    sweet chilli dipping sauce,
        to serve
For the filling
    4–6 Chinese dried mushrooms,
        soaked for 30 minutes in warm
        water to cover
    50g/2oz cellophane noodles
    30ml/2 tbsp vegetable oil
    2 garlic cloves, chopped
    2 fresh red chillies, seeded
        and chopped
    225g/8oz minced (ground) pork
    50g/2oz peeled cooked prawns
        (shrimp), thawed if frozen
    30ml/2 tbsp Thai fish sauce
    5ml/1 tsp granulated sugar
    1 carrot, grated
    50g/2oz piece of canned bamboo
        shoot, drained and chopped
    50g/2oz/⅔ cup beansprouts
    2 spring onions (scallions),
        finely chopped
    15ml/1 tbsp chopped fresh
        coriander (cilantro)
    ground black pepper

1 Make the filling. Drain the soaked
mushrooms. Cut off and discard the
stems, then chop the caps finely.

2 Place the noodles in a large bowl,
cover with boiling water and soak for
10 minutes. Drain the noodles and snip
them into 5cm/2in lengths.

3 Heat the oil in a wok, add the garlic
and chillies and stir-fry for 30 seconds.
Transfer to a plate. Add the pork to the
wok and stir-fry until it has browned.

4 Add the mushrooms, noodles and
prawns. Stir in the fish sauce and sugar,
then add pepper to taste.

5 Turn the mixture into a bowl. Stir in
the grated carrot, chopped bamboo
shoot, beansprouts, spring onions and
chopped coriander. Add the reserved
chilli mixture and mix well.

6 Unwrap the spring roll wrappers.
Cover them with a dampened dish towel
while you are making the rolls, so that
they do not dry out, and work on them
one at a time. Put the flour in a small
bowl and stir in a little water to make a
paste. Place a spoonful of the filling in
the centre of a spring roll wrapper.

7 Turn the bottom edge over to cover
the filling, then fold in the sides. Roll
up the wrapper almost to the top, then
brush the top edge with the flour paste
and seal. Fill the remaining wrappers.

8 Heat the oil in a wok to 190°C/375°F
or until a cube of bread browns in about
40 seconds. Fry the spring rolls, in
batches, until crisp and golden. Drain
on kitchen paper and serve hot with
sweet chilli dipping sauce.

Energy 74Kcal/310kJ; Protein 3.1g; Carbohydrate 7.2g, of which sugars 0.7g; Fat 3.8g, of which saturates 0.7g; Cholesterol 10mg; Calcium 13mg; Fibre 0.4g; Sodium 12mg.

FIERY TUNA SPRING ROLLS

THIS MODERN TAKE ON THE CLASSIC SPRING ROLL IS SUBSTANTIAL ENOUGH TO SERVE AS A MAIN COURSE WITH NOODLES AND STIR-FRIED GREENS. THE TUNA AND WASABI FILLING IS FANTASTIC.

SERVES FOUR

INGREDIENTS
- 1 large chunk of very fresh thick tuna steak
- 45ml/3 tbsp light soy sauce
- 30ml/2 tbsp wasabi
- 16 mangetout (snow peas), trimmed
- 8 spring roll wrappers
- sunflower oil, for deep-frying
- soft noodles and stir-fried Asian greens, to serve
- soy sauce and sweet chilli sauce, for dipping

1 Place the tuna on a board. Using a sharp knife cut it into eight slices, each measuring about 12 x 2.5cm/4½ x 1in.

2 Place the tuna in a large, non-metallic dish in a single layer. Mix together the soy sauce and the wasabi and spoon evenly over the fish. Cover and marinate for 10–15 minutes.

3 Meanwhile, blanch the mangetout in boiling water for about 1 minute, drain and refresh under cold water. Drain and pat dry with kitchen paper.

4 Place a spring roll wrapper on a clean work surface and place a piece of tuna on top, in the centre.

COOK'S TIP
It is important to cut the tuna into neat, even slices. Chilling it briefly in the freezer, and using a very sharp knife or cleaver, makes this easier to achieve.

5 Top the tuna with 2 mangetout and fold over the sides and roll up. Brush the edges of the wrappers to seal.

6 Repeat with the remaining tuna, mangetout and wrappers.

7 Fill a large wok one-third full with oil and heat to 180°C/350°F or until a cube of bread browns in 45 seconds. Working in batches, deep-fry the rolls for 1–2 minutes, until crisp and golden.

8 Drain the rolls on kitchen paper and serve immediately with soft noodles and Asian greens. Serve the spring rolls with side dishes of soy sauce and sweet chilli sauce for dipping.

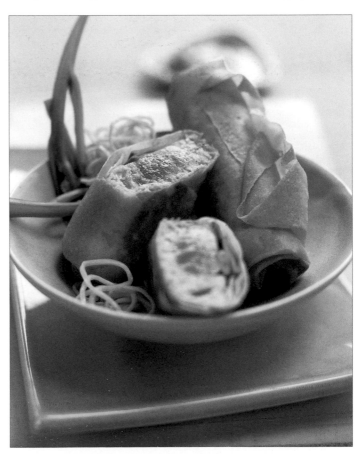

Energy 171Kcal/717kJ; Protein 14g; Carbohydrate 11.4g, of which sugars 1.7g; Fat 8g, of which saturates 1.3g; Cholesterol 14mg; Calcium 36mg; Fibre 0.8g; Sodium 825mg.

PEA AND POTATO PAKORAS WITH COCONUT AND MINT CHUTNEY

THESE DELICIOUS GOLDEN BITES ARE SOLD AS STREET FOOD THROUGHOUT INDIA. THEY MAKE A WONDERFUL SNACK DRIZZLED WITH THE FRAGRANT COCONUT AND MINT CHUTNEY.

MAKES TWENTY-FIVE

INGREDIENTS

15ml/1 tbsp sunflower oil
20ml/4 tsp cumin seeds
5ml/1 tsp black mustard seeds
1 small onion, finely chopped
10ml/2 tsp grated fresh root ginger
2 fresh green chillies, seeded and
   chopped
600g/1lb 6oz potatoes, peeled, diced
   and boiled until tender
200g/7oz fresh peas
juice of 1 lemon
90ml/6 tbsp chopped fresh coriander
   (cilantro) leaves
115g/4oz/1 cup gram flour
25g/1oz/¼ cup self-raising
   (self-rising) flour
40g/1½oz/⅓ cup rice flour
large pinch of ground turmeric
10ml/2 tsp crushed coriander seeds
350ml/12fl oz/1½ cups water
vegetable oil, for deep-frying
salt and ground black pepper
For the chutney
105ml/7 tbsp coconut cream
200ml/7fl oz/scant 1 cup natural
   (plain) yogurt
50g/2oz fresh mint leaves, finely
   chopped
5ml/1 tsp golden caster
   (superfine) sugar
juice of 1 lime

1 Heat a wok and add the sunflower oil. When hot, add the cumin and mustard seeds and stir-fry for 1–2 minutes.

2 Add the onion, ginger and chillies to the wok and cook for 3–4 minutes. Add the cooked potatoes, stir a few times, then add the peas and stir-fry for 3-4 minutes. Season, then stir in the lemon juice and coriander leaves.

COOK'S TIP
Gram flour is made from ground chickpeas and is widely used in Asian cooking. It is available in most large supermarkets and Asian stores.

3 To make the batter, put the gram flour, self-raising flour and rice flour in a bowl. Season and add the turmeric and coriander seeds. Gradually whisk in the water to make a smooth, thick batter.

4 To make the chutney, place all the ingredients in a blender and process until smooth. Season, then chill.

5 Leave the mixture to cool slightly, then divide into 25 portions. Shape each portion into a ball and chill. To cook the pakoras, fill a wok one-third full of oil and heat to 180ºC/350ºF. Working in batches, dip the balls in the batter, then drop into the oil and deep-fry for 1–2 minutes. Drain the pakoras on kitchen paper and serve with the chutney.

Energy 126Kcal/525kJ; Protein 4.1g; Carbohydrate 8.3g, of which sugars 2.6g; Fat 8.8g, of which saturates 5.2g; Cholesterol 0mg; Calcium 35mg; Fibre 1.3g; Sodium 16mg.

POTATO, SHALLOT AND GARLIC SAMOSAS WITH GREEN PEAS

MOST SAMOSAS ARE DEEP-FRIED. THESE ARE BAKED, ALTHOUGH THEIR FILLING IS MADE IN A WOK. THEY ARE PERFECT FOR PARTIES, SINCE THE PASTRIES NEED NO LAST-MINUTE ATTENTION.

MAKES TWENTY-FIVE

INGREDIENTS
1 large potato, about 250g/
 9oz, diced
15ml/1 tbsp groundnut
 (peanut) oil
2 shallots, finely chopped
1 garlic clove, finely chopped
60ml/4 tbsp coconut milk
5ml/1 tsp Thai red or green
 curry paste
75g/3oz/¾ cup peas
juice of ½ lime
25 samosa wrappers or 10 x 5cm/
 4 x 2in strips of filo pastry
salt and ground black pepper
oil, for brushing

1 Preheat the oven to 220°C/425°F/ Gas 7. Bring a small pan of water to the boil, add the diced potato, cover and cook for 10–15 minutes, until tender. Drain and set aside.

2 Meanwhile, heat the groundnut oil in a wok and cook the shallots and garlic over a medium heat, stirring occasionally, for 4–5 minutes, until softened and golden.

3 Add the drained diced potato, coconut milk, red or green curry paste, peas and lime juice to the wok. Mash together coarsely with a wooden spoon. Season to taste with salt and pepper and cook over a low heat for 2–3 minutes, then remove the pan from the heat and set aside until the mixture has cooled a little.

4 Lay a samosa wrapper or filo strip flat on the work surface. Brush with a little oil, then place a generous teaspoonful of the mixture in the middle of one end. Turn one corner diagonally over the filling to meet the long edge.

5 Continue folding over the filling, keeping the triangular shape as you work down the strip. Brush with a little more oil if necessary and place on a baking sheet. Prepare all the other samosas in the same way.

6 Bake for 15 minutes, or until the pastry is golden and crisp. Leave to cool slightly before serving.

COOK'S TIP
Many Asian food stores sell what is described as a samosa pad. This is a packet, usually frozen, containing about 50 oblong pieces of samosa pastry. Filo pastry, cut to size, can be used instead.

Energy 42Kcal/178kJ; Protein 1.2g; Carbohydrate 8.5g, of which sugars 0.6g; Fat 0.6g, of which saturates 0.1g; Cholesterol 0mg; Calcium 14mg; Fibre 0.5g; Sodium 4mg.

CORN FRITTERS

SOMETIMES IT IS THE SIMPLEST DISHES THAT TASTE THE BEST. THESE FRITTERS, PACKED WITH CRUNCHY CORN, ARE VERY EASY TO PREPARE AND COOK QUICKLY IN A HOT WOK.

MAKES TWELVE

INGREDIENTS

    3 corn cobs, total weight about
      250g/9oz
    1 garlic clove, crushed
    small bunch fresh coriander
      (cilantro), chopped
    1 small fresh red or green chilli,
      seeded and finely chopped
    1 spring onion (scallion),
      finely chopped
    15ml/1 tbsp soy sauce
    75g/3oz/⅔ cup rice flour or plain
      (all-purpose) flour
    2 eggs, lightly beaten
    60ml/4 tbsp water
    oil, for shallow-frying
    salt and ground black pepper
    sweet chilli sauce, to serve

1 Using a sharp knife, slice the kernels from the cobs and place them in a large bowl. Add the garlic, chopped coriander, red or green chilli, spring onion, soy sauce, flour, beaten eggs and water and mix well. Season with salt and pepper to taste and mix again. The mixture should be firm enough to hold its shape, but not stiff.

2 Heat the oil in a wok. Add spoonfuls of the corn mixture, gently spreading each one out with the back of the spoon to make a roundish fritter. Cook for 1–2 minutes on each side.

3 Drain on kitchen paper and keep hot while frying more fritters in the same way. Serve hot with sweet chilli sauce.

Energy 77Kcal/322kJ; Protein 2.3g; Carbohydrate 7.8g, of which sugars 0.6g; Fat 4.1g, of which saturates 0.6g; Cholesterol 32mg; Calcium 24mg; Fibre 0.8g; Sodium 104mg.

GREEN CURRY PUFFS

SHRIMP PASTE AND GREEN CURRY SAUCE, USED JUDICIOUSLY, GIVE THESE PUFFS THEIR DISTINCTIVE, SPICY, SAVOURY FLAVOUR, AND THE ADDITION OF CHILLI STEPS UP THE HEAT.

MAKES TWENTY-FOUR

INGREDIENTS
    24 small wonton wrappers, about
        8cm/3¼in square, thawed if frozen
    15ml/1 tbsp cornflour (cornstarch),
        mixed to a paste with 30ml/
        2 tbsp water
    oil, for deep-frying
For the filling
    1 small potato, about 115g/4oz,
        boiled and mashed
    25g/1oz/3 tbsp cooked petits pois
        (baby peas)
    25g/1oz/3 tbsp cooked corn
    few sprigs fresh coriander
        (cilantro), chopped
    1 small fresh red chilli, seeded and
        finely chopped
    ½ lemon grass stalk, finely chopped
    15ml/1 tbsp soy sauce
    5ml/1 tsp shrimp paste or fish sauce
    5ml/1 tsp Thai green curry paste

1 Combine the filling ingredients. Lay out one wonton wrapper and place a teaspoon of the filling in the centre.

2 Brush a little of the cornflour paste along two sides of the square. Fold the other two sides over to meet them, then press together to make a triangular pastry and seal in the filling. Make more pastries in the same way.

3 Heat the oil in a wok to 190°C/375°F or until a cube of bread, added to the oil, browns in about 40 seconds. Add the pastries to the oil, a few at a time, and fry them for about 5 minutes, until golden brown.

4 Remove from the wok and drain on kitchen paper. If you intend serving the puffs hot, place them in a low oven while cooking successive batches. The puffs also taste good cold

COOK'S TIP
Wonton wrappers dry out quickly, so keep them covered, using clear film (plastic wrap), until you are ready to use them.

Energy 69Kcal/291kJ; Protein 1.4g; Carbohydrate 9.9g, of which sugars 0.4g; Fat 3g, of which saturates 0.4g; Cholesterol 1mg; Calcium 22mg; Fibre 0.5g; Sodium 58mg.

STEAMED OYSTERS <u>WITH</u> ZESTY TOMATO <u>AND</u> CUCUMBER SALSA

A PLATE OF LIGHTLY STEAMED FRESH OYSTERS MAKES A DELICIOUS AND IMPRESSIVE APPETIZER FOR A SPECIAL OCCASION, AND IS EASY TO PREPARE. THE FRESH, ZESTY, AROMATIC SALSA COMPLEMENTS THE DELICATE FLAVOUR AND TEXTURE OF THE OYSTERS PERFECTLY, AND EACH IRRESISTIBLE MOUTHFUL FEELS LIKE THE ULTIMATE INDULGENCE.

SERVES FOUR

INGREDIENTS
    30ml/2 tbsp sunflower oil
    1 garlic clove, crushed
    15ml/1 tbsp light soy sauce
    12–16 oysters
    sea salt, to serve
For the salsa
    1 ripe plum tomato, seeds removed
    ½ small cucumber
    ¼ small red onion
    15ml/1 tbsp very finely chopped
        coriander (cilantro)
    1 small red chilli, seeded and very
        finely chopped
    juice of 1–2 limes
    salt and ground black pepper

1 First prepare the salsa. Finely dice the tomato, cucumber and red onion. Place in a bowl with the chopped coriander and red chilli.

2 Add the lime juice to the bowl and season to taste. Set aside (at room temperature) for 15–20 minutes.

3 In a separate bowl, mix together the sunflower oil, garlic and soy sauce.

COOK'S TIP
To de-seed the tomato, cut it in half around the middle rather than over the top, and then scoop out the seeds using a teaspoon.

4 Carefully open the oysters using a special oyster knife or a strong knife with a short, blunt blade. Arrange the oysters in their half shells in a bamboo steamer and spoon over the sauce.

5 Cover the steamer and place over a wok of simmering water. Steam the oysters for 2–3 minutes.

6 Arrange the oysters on a bed of sea salt, top each with a teaspoonful of the salsa and serve.

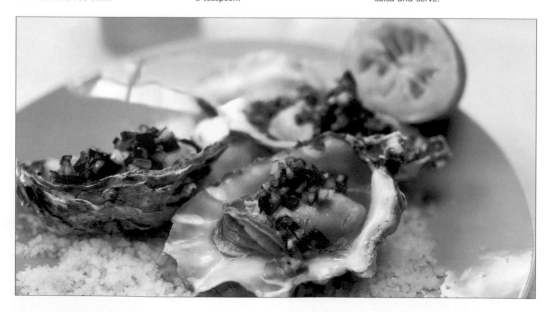

Energy 82Kcal/339kJ; Protein 4.5g; Carbohydrate 2.4g, of which sugars 1.3g; Fat 6.1g, of which saturates 0.8g; Cholesterol 21mg; Calcium 60mg; Fibre 0.4g; Sodium 461mg.

LEMON, CHILLI AND HERB STEAMED RAZOR CLAMS

RAZOR CLAMS HAVE BEAUTIFUL STRIPED GOLD AND BROWN TUBULAR SHELLS AND MAKE A WONDERFUL AND UNUSUAL APPETIZER. HERE THEY ARE LIGHTLY STEAMED AND TOSSED IN A FRAGRANT ITALIAN-STYLE DRESSING OF CHILLI, LEMON, GARLIC AND PARSLEY. SERVE WITH CRUSTY BREAD FOR MOPPING UP THE JUICES. FOR A MAIN COURSE, DOUBLE THE QUANTITY.

SERVES FOUR

INGREDIENTS
    12 razor clams
    90–120ml/6–8 tbsp extra virgin
      olive oil
    finely grated rind and juice of
      1 small lemon
    2 garlic cloves, very finely grated
    1 red chilli, seeded and very
      finely chopped
    60ml/4 tbsp chopped flat leaf parsley
    salt and ground black pepper
    mixed salad leaves and crusty bread,
      to serve

1 Wash the razor clams well in plenty of cold running water. Drain and arrange half the clams in a steamer, with the hinge side down.

2 Pour 5cm/2in water into a wok and bring to the boil. Carefully balance the steamer over the water and cover tightly. Steam for 3–4 minutes until the clams have opened.

3 Remove the clams from the wok and keep warm while you steam the remaining clams in the same way.

4 In a bowl, mix together the olive oil, grated lemon rind and juice, garlic, red chilli and flat leaf parsley.

5 Season the dressing well with salt and pepper. Spoon the mixture over the steamed razor clams on plates and serve immediately with a crisp mixed-leaf salad and crusty bread.

Energy 188Kcal/775kJ; Protein 6.1g; Carbohydrate 2.9g, of which sugars 0.5g; Fat 16.9g, of which saturates 2.4g; Cholesterol 20mg; Calcium 47mg; Fibre 1.1g; Sodium 364mg.

SEAWEED-WRAPPED PRAWN ROLLS

JAPANESE NORI SEAWEED IS USED TO ENCLOSE THE FRAGRANT FILLING OF PRAWNS, WATER CHESTNUTS, AND FRESH HERBS AND SPICES IN THESE PRETTY STEAMED ROLLS. IDEAL FOR ENTERTAINING, THE ROLLS CAN BE PREPARED IN ADVANCE AND STORED IN THE REFRIGERATOR UNTIL READY TO STEAM.

SERVES FOUR

INGREDIENTS

675g/1½lb raw tiger prawns (jumbo shrimp), peeled and deveined
5ml/1 tsp finely chopped kaffir lime leaves
1 red chilli, seeded and chopped
5ml/1 tsp finely grated garlic clove
5ml/1 tsp finely grated root ginger
5ml/1 tsp finely grated lime rind
60ml/4 tbsp very finely chopped fresh coriander (cilantro)
1 egg white, lightly beaten
30ml/2 tbsp chopped water chestnuts
4 sheets of nori
salt and ground black pepper
ketjap manis or soy sauce, to serve

1 Place the prawns in a food processor with the lime leaves, red chilli, garlic, ginger, lime rind and coriander. Process until smooth, add the egg white and water chestnuts, season and process again until combined. Transfer the mixture to a bowl, cover and chill for 3–4 hours.

2 Lay the nori sheets on a clean, dry surface and spread the prawn mixture over each sheet, leaving a 2cm/¾in border at one end. Roll up to form tight rolls, wrap in clear film (plastic wrap) and chill for 2–3 hours.

3 Unwrap the rolls and place on a board. Using a sharp knife, cut each roll into 2cm/¾in lengths. Place the slices in a baking parchment-lined bamboo steamer, cover and place over a wok of simmering water (making sure the water does not touch the steamer).

4 Steam the rolls for 6–8 minutes, or until cooked through. Serve warm or at room temperature with a dish of ketjap manis or soy sauce for dipping.

Energy 136Kcal/574kJ; Protein 30.8g; Carbohydrate 0.4g, of which sugars 0.4g; Fat 1.2g, of which saturates 0.2g; Cholesterol 329mg; Calcium 162mg; Fibre 0.7g; Sodium 345mg.

CRAB DIM SUM WITH CHINESE CHIVES

THESE DELECTABLE CHINESE-STYLE DUMPLINGS HAVE A WONDERFULLY STICKY TEXTURE AND MAKE A PERFECT APPETIZER. YOU CAN MAKE THEM IN ADVANCE, STORING THEM IN THE REFRIGERATOR UNTIL READY TO COOK. STEAM THEM JUST BEFORE SERVING, THEN ENJOY THE SENSATION AS YOUR TEETH SINK THROUGH THE SOFT WRAPPER INTO THE FILLING.

SERVES FOUR

INGREDIENTS
    150g/5oz fresh white crab meat
    115g/4oz minced (ground) pork
    30ml/2 tbsp chopped Chinese chives
    15ml/1 tbsp finely chopped red
      (bell) pepper
    30ml/2 tbsp sweet chilli sauce
    30ml/2 tbsp hoisin sauce
    24 fresh dumpling wrappers
      (available from Asian stores)
    Chinese chives, to garnish
    chilli oil and soy sauce, to serve

1 Place the crab meat, pork and chopped chives in a bowl. Add the red pepper, sweet chilli and hoisin sauces.

VARIATION
Use chopped raw tiger prawns (jumbo shrimp) in place of the crab.

2 Working with 2–3 wrappers at a time, put a spoonful of the mixture on to each wrapper. Brush the edges of a wrapper with water and fold over to form a half-moon shape. Press and pleat the edges to seal, and flatten. Cover with a clean, damp dish towel and make the rest.

3 Arrange the dumplings on 3 lightly oiled plates and fit inside 3 tiers of a bamboo steamer.

4 Cover the steamer and place over a wok of simmering water (making sure the water does not touch the steamer). Steam for 8–10 minutes, or until the dumplings are cooked through and become slightly translucent.

5 Divide the dumplings among four plates. Garnish with Chinese chives and serve immediately with chilli oil and soy sauce for dipping.

Energy 166Kcal/700kJ; Protein 14.7g; Carbohydrate 20.5g, of which sugars 1.4g; Fat 3.3g, of which saturates 1.1g; Cholesterol 46mg; Calcium 83mg; Fibre 0.8g; Sodium 287mg.

HERB AND CHILLI FISH CUSTARDS

THESE PRETTY LITTLE CUSTARDS MAKE AN UNUSUAL, BEAUTIFULLY PRESENTED AND RATHER EXOTIC APPETIZER FOR A DINNER PARTY, AND THEY COOK PERFECTLY IN THE WOK.

SERVES FOUR

INGREDIENTS

2 eggs
200ml/7fl oz/scant 1 cup
  coconut cream
60ml/4 tbsp chopped fresh
  coriander (cilantro)
1 fresh red chilli, seeded and sliced
15ml/1 tbsp finely chopped
  lemon grass
2 kaffir lime leaves, finely shredded
30ml/2 tbsp Thai red curry paste
1 garlic clove, crushed
5ml/1 tsp finely grated ginger
2 spring onions (scallions),
  finely sliced
300g/11oz mixed firm white fish fillets
  (cod, halibut or haddock), skinned
200g/7oz raw tiger prawns (jumbo
  shrimp), peeled and deveined
4–6 pandanus leaves
salt and ground black pepper
shredded cucumber, steamed rice
  and soy sauce, to serve

1 Beat the eggs in a bowl, then stir in the coconut cream, coriander, chilli, lemon grass, lime leaves, curry paste, garlic, ginger and spring onions. Finely chop the fish and roughly chop the prawns and add to the egg mixture. Stir well and season.

COOK'S TIP
Pandanus leaves keep the custards from drying out, and have a floral flavour that is transferred to the food, but they are not edible and should be discarded after the cooking.

2 Grease 4 ramekins and line them with the pandanus leaves. Divide the fish mixture between them, then arrange in a bamboo steamer.

3 Pour 5cm/2in water into a wok and bring to the boil. Suspend the steamer over the water, cover, reduce the heat to low and steam for 25–30 minutes, or until the fish is cooked through.

4 Serve the custards immediately with shredded cucumber, a little steamed rice and soy sauce.

Energy 150Kcal/632kJ; Protein 26.2g; Carbohydrate 2.8g, of which sugars 2.8g; Fat 3.9g, of which saturates 1g; Cholesterol 227mg; Calcium 100mg; Fibre 0.6g; Sodium 234mg.

FISH CAKES WITH CUCUMBER RELISH

THESE WONDERFUL SMALL FISH CAKES ARE A VERY FAMILIAR AND POPULAR APPETIZER IN THAILAND AND INCREASINGLY THROUGHOUT SOUTH-EAST ASIA. THEY ARE USUALLY SERVED WITH THAI BEER.

MAKES ABOUT TWELVE

INGREDIENTS
8 kaffir lime leaves
300g/11oz cod fillet, cut into chunks
30ml/2 tbsp Thai red curry paste
1 egg
30ml/2 tbsp Thai fish sauce
5ml/1 tsp granulated sugar
30ml/2 tbsp cornflour (cornstarch)
15ml/1 tbsp chopped fresh
   coriander (cilantro)
50g/2oz/½ cup green beans,
   thinly sliced
vegetable oil, for deep-frying
For the cucumber relish
60ml/4 tbsp coconut or rice vinegar
50g/2oz/¼ cup granulated sugar
60ml/4 tbsp water
1 head pickled garlic
1cm/½in piece fresh root
   ginger, peeled
1 cucumber, cut into thin batons
4 shallots, thinly sliced

1 Make the cucumber relish. Mix the coconut or rice vinegar, sugar and water in a small pan. Heat gently, stirring constantly until the sugar has completely dissolved. Remove the pan from the heat and leave to cool.

2 Separate the pickled garlic into cloves. Chop the cloves finely, along with the ginger, and place in a bowl. Add the cucumber batons and shallots, pour over the vinegar mixture and mix lightly. Cover and set aside.

3 Reserve five kaffir lime leaves for the garnish and thinly slice the remainder. Put the chunks of fish, curry paste and egg in a food processor and process to a smooth paste. Transfer the mixture to a bowl and stir in the fish sauce, sugar, cornflour, sliced kaffir lime leaves, coriander and green beans. Mix well, then shape the mixture into about twelve 5mm/¼in thick cakes, each measuring about 5cm/2in in diameter.

4 Heat the oil in a wok to 190°C/375°F or until a cube of bread, added to the oil, browns in about 40 seconds. Fry the fish cakes, a few at a time, for about 4–5 minutes, until cooked and evenly brown.

5 Lift out the fish cakes and drain them on kitchen paper. Keep each batch hot while frying successive batches. Garnish with the reserved kaffir lime leaves and serve with the cucumber relish.

Energy 83Kcal/346kJ; Protein 5.5g; Carbohydrate 5.8g, of which sugars 5.6g; Fat 4.4g, of which saturates 0.6g; Cholesterol 27mg; Calcium 15mg; Fibre 0.3g; Sodium 111mg.

SALMON, SESAME <u>AND</u> GINGER FISH CAKES

THESE LIGHT FISH CAKES ARE SCENTED WITH THE EXOTIC FLAVOURS OF SESAME, LIME AND GINGER. THEY MAKE A TEMPTING APPETIZER SERVED SIMPLY WITH A WEDGE OF LIME FOR SQUEEZING OVER, BUT ARE ALSO PERFECT FOR A LIGHT LUNCH OR SUPPER, SERVED WITH A CRUNCHY, REFRESHING SALAD.

MAKES TWENTY-FIVE

INGREDIENTS
  500g/1¼lb salmon fillet,
    skinned and boned
  45ml/3 tbsp dried breadcrumbs
  30ml/2 tbsp mayonnaise
  30ml/2 tbsp sesame seeds
  30ml/2 tbsp light soy sauce
  finely grated rind of 2 limes
  10ml/2 tsp finely grated
    fresh root ginger
  4 spring onions (scallions),
    finely sliced
  vegetable oil, for frying
  salt and ground black pepper
  spring onions (scallions), to garnish
  lime wedges, to serve

1 Finely chop the salmon and place in a bowl. Add the breadcrumbs, mayonnaise, sesame seeds, soy sauce, lime rind, ginger and spring onions and use your fingers to mix well.

2 With wet hands, divide the mixture into 25 portions and shape each into a small round cake. Place the cakes on a baking sheet, lined with baking parchment, cover and chill for at least two hours. They can be left overnight.

3 When you are ready to cook the fish cakes, heat about 5cm/2in vegetable oil in a wok and fry the fish cakes in batches, over a medium heat, for 2–3 minutes on each side.

4 Drain the fish cakes well on kitchen paper and serve warm or at room temperature, garnished with spring onion slivers and plenty of lime wedges for squeezing over.

Energy 83Kcal/343kJ; Protein 4.6g; Carbohydrate 1.6g, of which sugars 0.2g; Fat 6.5g, of which saturates 0.9g; Cholesterol 11mg; Calcium 16mg; Fibre 0.2g; Sodium 117mg.

LETTUCE PARCELS

KNOWN AS SANG CHOY IN HONG KONG, THIS IS A POPULAR "ASSEMBLE-IT-YOURSELF" TREAT. THE FILLING — AN IMAGINATIVE BLEND OF TEXTURES AND FLAVOURS — IS SERVED WITH CRISP LETTUCE LEAVES, WHICH ARE SPREAD WITH HOISIN SAUCE AND USED AS WRAPPERS.

SERVES SIX

INGREDIENTS

2 boneless chicken breast portions, total weight about 350g/12oz
4 Chinese dried mushrooms, soaked for 30 minutes in warm water to cover
30ml/2 tbsp vegetable oil
2 garlic cloves, crushed
6 drained canned water chestnuts, thinly sliced
30ml/2 tbsp light soy sauce
5ml/1 tsp Sichuan peppercorns, dry fried and crushed
4 spring onions (scallions), finely chopped
5ml/1 tsp sesame oil
vegetable oil, for deep-frying
50g/2oz cellophane noodles
salt and ground black pepper (optional)
1 crisp lettuce and 60ml/4 tbsp hoisin sauce, to serve

1 Remove the skin from the chicken breasts, pat dry and set aside. Chop the chicken into thin strips. Drain the soaked mushrooms. Cut off and discard the mushroom stems; slice the caps finely and set aside.

2 Heat the oil in a wok. Add the garlic, then add the chicken and stir-fry until the pieces are cooked through and no longer pink. Check by lifting one of the thicker chicken strips out of the wok and cutting it in half.

3 Add the sliced mushrooms, water chestnuts, soy sauce and peppercorns. Toss for 2–3 minutes, then season, if needed. Stir in half of the spring onions, then the sesame oil. Remove from the heat and keep warm.

4 Heat the oil for deep-frying to 190°C/375°F. Cut the chicken skin into strips, deep-fry until very crisp and drain on kitchen paper. Add the noodles to the hot oil, deep-fry until crisp. Transfer to a plate lined with kitchen paper.

5 Crush the noodles and put in a serving dish. Top with the chicken skin, chicken mixture and the remaining spring onions. Arrange the lettuce leaves on a large platter.

6 Toss the chicken and noodles to mix. Invite guests to take one or two lettuce leaves, spread the inside with hoisin sauce and add a spoonful of filling, turning in the sides of the leaves and rolling them into a parcel. The parcels are traditionally eaten in the hand.

Energy 195Kcal/821kJ; Protein 28.7g; Carbohydrate 7.5g, of which sugars 0.6g; Fat 5.5g, of which saturates 0.9g; Cholesterol 82mg; Calcium 11mg; Fibre 0.1g; Sodium 428mg.

STEAMED PORK BUNS

THESE DELICIOUSLY LIGHT STUFFED BUNS ARE A POPULAR STREET
SNACK SOLD THROUGHOUT CHINA. THE SOFT TEXTURE OF THE BUN
CONTRASTS WONDERFULLY WITH THE SPICED MEAT FILLING INSIDE.
THEY MAKE AN UNUSUAL ALTERNATIVE TO RICE AND, ONCE
COOKED, CAN BE REHEATED IN THE STEAMER.

SERVES FOUR

INGREDIENTS
   30ml/2 tbsp golden caster
    (superfine) sugar
   10ml/2 tsp dried yeast
   300g/11oz/2¾ cups plain
    (all-purpose) flour
   30ml/2 tbsp sunflower oil
   10ml/2 tsp baking powder
For the filling
   250g/9oz pork sausages
   15ml/1 tbsp barbecue sauce
   30ml/2 tbsp oyster sauce
   15ml/1 tbsp sweet chilli sauce
   15ml/1 tbsp Chinese rice wine
   15ml/1 tbsp hoisin sauce
   5ml/1 tsp chilli oil

1 To make the dough pour 250ml/
8fl oz/1 cup warm water into a mixing
bowl. Add the sugar and stir to dissolve.
Stir in the yeast, cover and leave in a
warm place for 15 minutes.

2 Sift the flour into a large mixing bowl
and make a well in the centre. Add the
sugar and yeast mixture to it with the
sunflower oil. Stir the mixture together
using your fingers and turn out on to a
lightly floured surface.

3 Knead the dough for 8–10 minutes
until smooth and elastic. Place in a
lightly oiled bowl, cover with a dish
towel and leave to rise in a warm place
for 3–4 hours.

4 When risen, place the dough on a
lightly floured surface, punch down and
shape into a large circle. Sprinkle the
baking powder in the centre, bring all
the edges towards the centre and knead
for 6–8 minutes. Divide the dough into
12 balls, cover with a clean, damp dish
towel and set aside.

5 Squeeze the sausage meat from the
casings into a large bowl and stir in
the barbecue sauce, oyster sauce,
sweet chilli sauce, rice wine, hoisin
sauce and chilli oil. Mix thoroughly,
using your fingers to combine.

6 Press each dough ball to form a
round, 12cm/4½in in diameter. Place a
large spoonful of the pork mixture in the
centre of each round and bring the
edges up to the centre, press together
to seal and form a bun shape.

7 Arrange the buns on several layers of
a large bamboo steamer, cover and
steam over a wok of simmering water
for 20–25 minutes, or until they are
puffed up and the pork is cooked
through. Serve immediately.

VARIATION
You can replace the sausage meat with
cooked, peeled prawns (shrimp). Place
the same quantity of prawns in a food
blender and process with the other
ingredients until you have a rough paste.

Energy 588Kcal/2468kJ; Protein 14g; Carbohydrate 76.4g, of which sugars 14g; Fat 27.3g, of which saturates 8.5g;
Cholesterol 29mg; Calcium 137mg; Fibre 2.8g; Sodium 722mg.

STUFFED THAI OMELETTES

OMELETTES ARE USUALLY COOKED IN A FLAT PAN, BUT A WOK WORKS EQUALLY WELL. THE HOT CHILLI IN THIS RECIPE MAKES AN INTERESTING CONTRASTING FLAVOUR TO THE DELICATE EGG.

3 To make the omelettes, put the eggs and Thai fish sauce in a bowl and beat together lightly with a fork.

4 Heat 15ml/1 tbsp of the oil in an omelette pan or wok over a medium heat. When the oil is very hot, but not smoking, add half the beaten egg mixture and immediately tilt the pan or wok to spread the egg into a thin, even layer over the base. Cook over a medium heat until the omelette is just set and the underside is golden.

SERVES FOUR

INGREDIENTS
    30ml/2 tbsp groundnut
        (peanut) oil
    2 garlic cloves, finely chopped
    1 small onion, finely chopped
    225g/8oz minced (ground) pork
    30ml/2 tbsp Thai fish sauce
    5ml/1 tsp granulated sugar
    2 tomatoes, peeled and chopped
    15ml/1 tbsp chopped fresh
        coriander (cilantro)
    ground black pepper
    fresh coriander (cilantro)
        sprigs and sliced fresh red
        chillies, to garnish
For the omelettes
    5 eggs
    15ml/1 tbsp Thai fish sauce
    30ml/2 tbsp groundnut
        (peanut) oil

1 Heat the oil in a wok, add the garlic and onion, and cook over a medium heat, for 3–4 minutes, until soft. Add the pork and cook until lightly browned.

2 Stir in the Thai fish sauce, sugar and tomatoes, season with pepper and simmer over a low heat until thickened. Mix in the coriander. Remove the wok from the heat, cover to keep warm and set aside while you make the omelettes.

5 Spoon half the filling into the centre of the omelette. Fold into a neat square parcel by bringing the opposite sides of the omelette towards each other. Slide the parcel on to a serving dish, folded side down. Make another omelette parcel in the same way. Garnish with the coriander sprigs and chillies. Cut each omelette in half to serve.

COOK'S TIP
Making the omelette in a wok is actually easier than in a regular frying pan, since the sloping sides make it simple to flip the omelette over the filling.

Energy 305Kcal/1267kJ; Protein 19.2g; Carbohydrate 4.8g, of which sugars 4.5g; Fat 23.6g, of which saturates 5.7g; Cholesterol 275mg; Calcium 48mg; Fibre 0.7g; Sodium 130mg.

GOLDEN CORN CAKES WITH AIOLI

EAST MEETS WEST IN THESE CRISP, MOUTHWATERING CAKES THAT BRING TOGETHER CREAMY GOAT'S CHEESE AND TANGY MEDITERRANEAN PEPPERS IN THE ASIAN WOK.

SERVES FOUR

INGREDIENTS
  300g/11oz/scant 2 cups fresh
    corn kernels
  200g/7oz/scant 1 cup ricotta cheese
  200g/7oz/scant 1 cup goat's
    cheese, crumbled
  30ml/2 tbsp thyme leaves
  50g/2oz/¹⁄₂ cup plain
    (all-purpose) flour
  1 large (US extra large) egg,
    lightly beaten
  150g/5oz natural dried breadcrumbs
  vegetable oil, for deep-frying
  salt and ground black pepper
For the aioli
  2 red (bell) peppers, halved
    and seeded
  2 garlic cloves, crushed
  250ml/8fl oz/1 cup mayonnaise

1 Make the aioli. Preheat the grill (broiler) to medium-high and cook the peppers, skin-side up, for 8–10 minutes, until the skins blister. Place the peppers in a plastic bag for 10 minutes and then peel away the skin. Place the flesh in a food processor with the garlic and mayonnaise and blend until fairly smooth. Transfer to a bowl and chill.

2 In a bowl, combine the corn, cheeses and thyme, then stir in the flour and egg and season well.

COOK'S TIP
If you're short on time, make the aioli with bottled peppers.

3 Place the breadcrumbs on a plate. Roll 15ml/1 tbsp of the corn mixture into a ball, flatten slightly and coat in the breadcrumbs. Place on baking parchment and chill for 30 minutes.

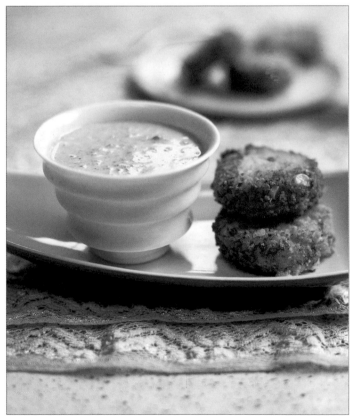

4 Fill a wok one-third full of oil and heat to 180°C/350°F (or until a cube of bread, dropped into the oil, browns in 45 seconds). Working in batches, deep-fry the corn cakes for 1–2 minutes, until golden. Drain well on kitchen paper and serve with the aioli.

COOK'S TIP
If you deep-fry regularly, you will soon learn to judge when the oil has reached optimum temperature. If you need reassurance, buy a deep-fat thermometer. The safest and most reliable are those that can be clipped to the side of the wok before the oil is hot.

Energy 1048Kcal/4363kJ; Protein 26.1g; Carbohydrate 68.2g, of which sugars 17.3g; Fat 76.5g, of which saturates 22g; Cholesterol 162mg; Calcium 156mg; Fibre 3.9g; Sodium 1091mg.

THAI TEMPEH CAKES WITH DIPPING SAUCE

MADE FROM SOYA BEANS, TEMPEH IS SIMILAR TO TOFU BUT HAS A NUTTIER TASTE. HERE, IT IS COMBINED WITH A FRAGRANT BLEND OF LEMON GRASS, CORIANDER AND GINGER TO MAKE TASTY LITTLE RISSOLES THAT GO VERY WELL WITH THE LIGHT DIPPING SAUCE THAT ACCOMPANIES THEM.

MAKES EIGHT

INGREDIENTS

    1 lemon grass stalk, outer leaves
       removed and inside finely chopped
    2 garlic cloves, chopped
    2 spring onions (scallions),
       finely chopped
    2 shallots, finely chopped
    2 fresh red chillies, seeded and
       finely chopped
    2.5cm/1in piece fresh root ginger,
       finely chopped
    60ml/4 tbsp chopped fresh coriander
       (cilantro), plus extra to garnish
    250g/9oz/2¼ cups tempeh, thawed if
       frozen, sliced
    15ml/1 tbsp fresh lime juice
    5ml/1 tsp granulated sugar
    45ml/3 tbsp plain (all-purpose) flour
    1 large (US extra large) egg,
       lightly beaten
    salt and freshly ground black pepper
    vegetable oil, for frying
For the dipping sauce
    45ml/3 tbsp mirin (see Cook's Tip)
    45ml/3 tbsp white wine vinegar
    2 spring onions (scallions),
       thinly sliced
    15ml/1 tbsp granulated sugar
    2 fresh red chillies, seeded and
       finely chopped
    30ml/2 tbsp chopped fresh
       coriander (cilantro)
    large pinch of salt

1 Make the dipping sauce. Mix together the mirin, vinegar, spring onions, sugar, chillies, coriander and salt in a small bowl. Cover with clear film (plastic wrap) and set aside until ready to serve.

COOK'S TIP

Mirin is a sweet rice wine from Japan. It has quite a delicate flavour and is used for cooking. Rice wine for drinking, called sake, is rather more expensive. Both are available from Asian food stores. If you cannot locate mirin, dry sherry can be used instead, although the results will not be quite the same.

2 Place the lemon grass, garlic, spring onions, shallots, chillies, ginger and coriander in a food processor or blender, then process to a coarse paste. Add the tempeh, lime juice and sugar and process until combined. Add the flour and egg, with salt and pepper to taste. Process again until the mixture forms a coarse, sticky paste.

3 Scrape the paste into a bowl. Take one-eighth of the mixture at a time and form it into rounds with your hands.

4 Heat a little oil in a wok, then fry the tempeh cakes for 5–6 minutes, turning once, until golden. Drain on kitchen paper. Transfer to a platter, garnish and serve with the sauce.

Energy 79Kcal/332kJ; Protein 4.5g; Carbohydrate 9.1g, of which sugars 4.3g; Fat 2.3g, of which saturates 0.4g; Cholesterol 26mg; Calcium 192mg; Fibre 0.8g; Sodium 15mg.

SON-IN-LAW EGGS

THE FASCINATING NAME FOR THIS DISH COMES FROM A STORY ABOUT A PROSPECTIVE BRIDEGROOM WHO VERY MUCH WANTED TO IMPRESS HIS FUTURE MOTHER-IN-LAW AND DEVISED A NEW RECIPE BASED ON THE ONLY DISH HE KNEW HOW TO MAKE — BOILED EGGS.

SERVES FOUR TO SIX

INGREDIENTS
- 30ml/2 tbsp vegetable oil
- 6 shallots, thinly sliced
- 6 garlic cloves, thinly sliced
- 6 fresh red chillies, sliced
- oil, for deep-frying
- 6 hard-boiled eggs, shelled
- salad leaves, to serve
- sprigs of fresh coriander (cilantro), to garnish

For the sauce
- 75g/3oz/6 tbsp palm sugar or light muscovado (brown) sugar
- 75ml/5 tbsp Thai fish sauce
- 90ml/6 tbsp tamarind paste mixed with a little warm water

COOK'S TIP
Chillies' heat depends on which type is used and whether you include the seeds.

1 Make the sauce. Put the sugar, fish sauce and tamarind juice in a pan. Bring to the boil, stirring until the sugar dissolves, lower the heat and simmer for 5 minutes. Taste and add more sugar, fish sauce or tamarind juice, if needed. Transfer the sauce to a bowl.

2 Heat the vegetable oil in a frying pan and cook the shallots, garlic and chillies for 5 minutes. Transfer to a bowl.

3 Heat the oil in a wok to 190°C/375°F or until a cube of bread, added to the oil, browns in about 40 seconds. Deep-fry the eggs until golden. Remove and drain on kitchen paper.

4 Cut the eggs in quarters and arrange them on a bed of leaves. Drizzle with the sauce and sprinkle over the shallot mixture. Garnish with coriander sprigs and serve immediately.

Energy 180Kcal/752kJ; Protein 7.3g; Carbohydrate 18g, of which sugars 17.1g; Fat 9.4g, of which saturates 2g; Cholesterol 190mg; Calcium 50mg; Fibre 0.5g; Sodium 666mg.

RICE PAPER PARCELS WITH WILTED CHOI SUM

TRANSLUCENT RICE PAPER MAKES A WONDERFULLY CRISP WRAPPING FOR THE LIGHTLY SPICED VEGETABLE AND TOFU FILLING. TAKE CARE, AS THE PAPERS ARE VERY BRITTLE AND EASILY DAMAGED.

SERVES FOUR

INGREDIENTS

30ml/2 tbsp sunflower oil
90g/3½oz shiitake mushrooms, stalks
   discarded and finely chopped
30ml/2 tbsp chopped garlic
90g/3½oz water chestnuts,
   finely chopped
90g/3½oz firm tofu, finely chopped
2 spring onions (scallions),
   finely chopped
½ red (bell) pepper, seeded and
   finely chopped
50g/2oz mangetouts (snow peas),
   finely chopped
15ml/1 tbsp light soy sauce
15ml/1 tbsp sweet chilli sauce
45ml/3 tbsp chopped fresh
   coriander (cilantro)
30ml/2 tbsp chopped fresh
   mint leaves
90ml/6 tbsp plain
   (all-purpose) flour
12 medium rice paper wrappers
sunflower oil, for deep-frying
500g/1¼lb choi sum or Chinese
   greens, roughly sliced or chopped
egg fried rice, to serve

1 Heat the oil in a large wok over a high heat and add the chopped mushrooms. Stir-fry for 3–4 minutes, add the garlic and fry for 1 minute.

2 Add the water chestnuts, tofu, spring onions, red pepper and mangetout to the wok, and stir-fry for 2–3 minutes.

3 Add the soy and sweet chilli sauces to the wok. Remove from the heat and stir in the chopped coriander and mint. Leave to cool completely.

4 Place the flour in a bowl and stir in 105ml/7 tbsp of cold water to make a thick, smooth paste.

5 Fill a large bowl with warm water and dip a rice paper wrapper in it for a few minutes until softened. Remove and drain on a dish towel.

6 Divide the filling into 12 portions and spoon one portion on to the softened rice wrapper. Fold in each side and roll up tightly. Seal the ends with a little of the flour paste. Repeat with the remaining wrappers and filling.

7 Fill a wok one-third full with the oil and heat to 180°C/350°F or until a cube of bread, dropped into the oil, browns in 40 seconds. Working in batches of 2–3, deep-fry the parcels for 3 minutes until crisp and lightly browned. Drain well on kitchen paper and keep warm.

8 Pour off most of the oil, reserving 30ml/2 tbsp. Place the wok over a medium heat and add the choi sum. Stir-fry for 3–4 minutes. Divide among four warmed bowls and top with the parcels. Serve immediately with egg fried rice.

Energy 252Kcal/1051kJ; Protein 10.2g; Carbohydrate 34.6g, of which sugars 6.6g; Fat 8.5g, of which saturates 1g;
Cholesterol 0mg; Calcium 448mg; Fibre 6.8g; Sodium 313mg.

MEAT AND POULTRY DISHES

Rich meat curries and gently simmered dishes lend themselves perfectly to wok cooking, with great depths of flavour coming from ingredients such as chillies, garlic, shallots, ginger or galangal. Fresh lemon grass and coriander are often included, and smooth, sweet coconut milk is often the liquid that marries these robust tastes together and tames their stridency. From this chapter try Beef Rendang for a typically intense dish, or you could opt for a milder dish such as Thai Fried Rice, or the delicately aromatic Lemon and Sesame Chicken.

Lemon and Sesame Chicken

*THESE DELICATE STRIPS OF CHICKEN ARE AT THEIR BEST IF YOU
HAVE TIME TO LEAVE THEM TO MARINATE OVERNIGHT SO THAT
THEY CAN REALLY SOAK UP THE FLAVOURS. THE SUBTLE FRAGRANCE
OF LEMON PERFECTLY COMPLEMENTS THE RICH TASTE OF FRIED
CHICKEN AND THE NUTTY SESAME SEEDS.*

SERVES FOUR

INGREDIENTS
    4 large chicken breast portions,
      skinned and cut into strips
    15ml/1 tbsp light soy sauce
    15ml/1 tbsp Chinese rice wine
    2 garlic cloves, crushed
    10ml/2 tsp finely grated fresh
      root ginger
    1 egg, lightly beaten
    150g/5oz cornflour (cornstarch)
    sunflower oil, for deep-frying
    toasted sesame seeds, to sprinkle
    rice or noodles, to serve
For the sauce
    15ml/1 tbsp sunflower oil
    2 spring onions (scallions),
      finely sliced
    1 garlic clove, crushed
    10ml/2 tsp cornflour (cornstarch)
    90ml/6 tbsp chicken stock
    10ml/2 tsp finely grated lemon rind
    30ml/2 tbsp lemon juice
    10ml/2 tsp sugar
    2.5ml/½ tsp sesame oil
    salt

1 Place the chicken strips in a large,
non-metallic bowl. Mix together the light
soy sauce, rice wine, garlic and ginger
and pour over the chicken. Toss
together to combine.

2 Cover the bowl of chicken with clear
film (plastic wrap) and place in the
refrigerator overnight or for 8–10 hours,
if possible.

3 When ready to cook, add the beaten
egg to the chicken and mix well, then
tip the mixture into a colander to drain
off any excess marinade and egg.

4 Place the cornflour in a large plastic
bag and add the chicken pieces. Shake
it vigorously to coat the chicken strips
thoroughly.

5 Fill a wok one-third full of sunflower
oil and heat to 180ºC/350ºF (or until a
cube of bread, dropped into the oil,
browns in 45 seconds).

6 Deep-fry the chicken, in batches,
for 3–4 minutes. Lift out the chicken
using a slotted spoon and drain on
kitchen paper. Reheat the oil and deep-
fry the chicken once more, in batches,
for 2–3 minutes. Remove with a slotted
spoon and drain on kitchen paper. Pour
the oil out and wipe out the wok with
kitchen paper.

7 To make the sauce, heat the wok,
then add the sunflower oil. When the oil
is hot add the spring onions and garlic
and stir-fry for 1–2 minutes. Mix
together the cornflour, stock, lemon rind
and juice, sugar, sesame oil and salt
and pour into the wok.

8 Cook over a high heat for 2–3 minutes
until thickened. Return the chicken to
the wok, toss lightly to coat with sauce,
and sprinkle over the toasted sesame
seeds. Serve with rice or noodles.

Energy 229Kcal/959kJ; Protein 31.3g; Carbohydrate 4.3g, of which sugars 3.4g; Fat 9.7g, of which saturates 1.4g;
Cholesterol 94mg; Calcium 32mg; Fibre 0.5g; Sodium 397mg.

CASHEW CHICKEN

ONE OF THE MOST POPULAR ITEMS ON ANY CHINESE RESTAURANT MENU, CASHEW CHICKEN IS EASY TO RECREATE AT HOME. IT IS IMPORTANT TO HAVE THE WOK VERY HOT BEFORE ADDING THE CHICKEN OR IT WILL STEW RATHER THAN STIR-FRY. A CARBON STEEL WOK WILL GIVE GOOD RESULTS.

SERVES FOUR TO SIX

INGREDIENTS
  450g/1lb skinless chicken breast
    fillets
  1 red (bell) pepper
  2 garlic cloves
  4 dried red chillies
  30ml/2 tbsp vegetable oil
  30ml/2 tbsp oyster sauce
  15ml/1 tbsp soy sauce
  pinch of sugar
  1 bunch spring onions (scallions), cut
    into 5cm/2in lengths
  175g/6oz/1½ cups cashews, roasted
  coriander (cilantro) leaves,
    to garnish

1 Remove and discard the skin from the chicken breasts and trim off any excess fat. With a sharp knife, cut the chicken into bitesize pieces and set aside.

2 Halve the red pepper, scrape out the seeds and membranes and discard, then cut the flesh into 2cm/¾in dice. Peel and thinly slice the garlic and chop the dried red chillies.

3 Preheat a wok and then heat the oil. The best way to do this is to drizzle a "necklace" of oil around the inner rim of the wok, so that it drops down to coat the entire inner surface. Make sure the coating is even by swirling the wok.

4 Add the garlic and dried chillies to the wok and stir-fry over a medium heat until golden. Do not let the garlic burn, otherwise it will taste bitter.

5 Add the chicken to the wok and stir-fry until it is cooked through, then add the red pepper. If the mixture is very dry, add a little water.

6 Stir in the oyster sauce, soy sauce and sugar. Add the spring onions and cashew nuts. Stir-fry for 1–2 minutes more, until heated through. Spoon into a warm dish and serve immediately, garnished with the coriander leaves.

COOK'S TIP
Cashews are also valued for the "fruit" under which each nut grows. Although they are known as cashew apples, these so-called fruits are actually bulbous portions of the stem. They may be pink, red or yellow in colour and the crisp, sweet flesh can be eaten raw or made into a refreshing drink. Cashew apples – and undried nuts – are rarely seen outside their growing regions.

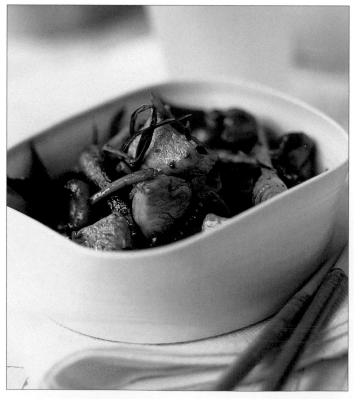

Energy 314Kcal/1307kJ; Protein 24.7g; Carbohydrate 10.2g, of which sugars 6.2g; Fat 19.6g, of which saturates 3.7g; Cholesterol 53mg; Calcium 24mg; Fibre 1.7g; Sodium 268mg.

ADOBO OF CHICKEN AND PORK

FOUR INGREDIENTS ARE ESSENTIAL IN AN ADOBO, ONE OF THE BEST-LOVED RECIPES IN THE FILIPINO REPERTOIRE. THEY ARE VINEGAR, GARLIC, PEPPERCORNS AND BAY LEAVES. THE PLANTAIN CHIPS ARE THE TRADITIONAL ACCOMPANIMENT BUT SWEET POTATO CHIPS CAN BE SERVED INSTEAD.

SERVES FOUR

INGREDIENTS

    1 chicken, about 1.4kg/3lb, or
      4 chicken quarters
    350g/12oz pork leg steaks (with fat)
    10ml/2 tsp sugar
    60ml/4 tbsp sunflower oil
    75ml/5 tbsp wine vinegar or cider
      vinegar
    4 plump garlic cloves, crushed
    1/2 tsp black peppercorns,
      crushed lightly
    15ml/1 tbsp light soy sauce
    4 bay leaves
    2.5ml/1/2 tsp annatto seeds, soaked
      in 30ml/2 tbsp boiling water, or
      2.5ml/1/2 tsp ground turmeric
    salt
For the plantain chips
    1–2 large plantains and/or
      1 sweet potato
    vegetable oil, for deep-frying

3 Add the vinegar, garlic, peppercorns, soy sauce and bay leaves and stir well. Strain the annatto seed liquid and stir it into the wok, stir in the turmeric. Add salt to taste. Bring to the boil, cover, lower the heat and simmer the chicken for 30–35 minutes. When the chicken is cooked through, remove the lid and simmer for 10 minutes more to reduce the liquid a little.

4 Meanwhile, prepare the plaintain chips. Heat the oil in a wok or deep-fryer to 195°C/390°F. Peel the plantains and slice them into rounds or chips. Deep-fry them, in batches if necessary, until cooked but not brown. Drain on kitchen paper. When ready to serve, reheat the oil and refry the plantains until crisp – it will take only seconds. Drain and serve with the adobo.

1 Wipe the chicken and cut into eight even-size pieces, or halve the chicken quarters, if using. Cut the pork into neat pieces. Spread out all the meat on a board, sprinkle lightly with sugar and set aside.

2 Heat the oil in a wok and fry the chicken and pork pieces, in batches if necessary, until they are golden.

COOK'S TIP
Sprinkling the chicken lightly with sugar turns the skin beautifully brown when fried, but do not have the oil too hot to begin with or they will over-brown.

Energy 676Kcal/2825kJ; Protein 60.2g; Carbohydrate 28.8g, of which sugars 8.1g; Fat 36.2g, of which saturates 6g; Cholesterol 178mg; Calcium 38mg; Fibre 1.7g; Sodium 503mg.

CHICKEN RENDANG

THIS SPICY RECIPE MAKES A MARVELLOUS DISH FOR A BUFFET. SERVE IT WITH PRAWN CRACKERS OR WITH BOILED RICE AND DEEP-FRIED ANCHOVIES, ACAR PICKLE OR A SELECTION OF SAMBALS.

SERVES FOUR

INGREDIENTS

1 chicken, about 1.4kg/3lb
5ml/1 tsp sugar
75g/3oz/1 cup desiccated (dry, unsweeted, shredded) coconut
4 small red or white onions, roughly chopped
2 garlic cloves, chopped
2.5cm/1in piece fresh root ginger, peeled and sliced
1–2 lemon grass stalks, root trimmed
2.5cm/1in piece fresh galangal, peeled and sliced
75ml/5 tbsp groundnut (peanut) oil or vegetable oil
10–15ml/2–3 tsp chilli powder, or to taste
400ml/14fl oz can coconut milk
10ml/2 tsp salt
fresh chives and deep-fried anchovies, to garnish

1 Joint the chicken into 8 pieces and remove the skin, sprinkle with the sugar and leave to stand for 1 hour.

2 Dry-fry the coconut in a wok or large frying pan over medium to low heat, turning all the time until it is crisp and golden. Place the fried coconut in a food processor and process to an oily paste. Transfer to a bowl and reserve.

3 Add the onions, garlic and ginger to the processor. Cut off the lower 5cm/2in of the lemon grass, chop and add to the processor with the galangal. Process to a fine paste.

4 Heat the oil in a wok or large pan and fry the onion mixture for a few minutes. Reduce the heat, stir in the chilli powder and cook for 2–3 minutes, stirring constantly. Spoon in 120ml/4fl oz/½ cup of the coconut milk and add salt to taste.

5 As soon as the mixture bubbles, add the chicken pieces, turning them until they are well coated with the spices. Pour in the remaining coconut milk, stirring constantly to prevent curdling.

6 Bruise the top of the lemon grass stalks and add to the wok or pan. Cover and cook gently for 40–45 minutes until the chicken is tender.

7 Just before serving, stir in the coconut paste. Bring to just below boiling point, then simmer for 5 minutes. Transfer to a serving bowl and garnish with fresh chives and deep-fried anchovies.

Energy 501Kcal/2098kJ; Protein 55.4g; Carbohydrate 7.2g, of which sugars 7.2g; Fat 28.1g, of which saturates 12.5g; Cholesterol 158mg; Calcium 45mg; Fibre 2.6g; Sodium 1233mg.

TANGY CHICKEN SALAD

WHEN YOU'VE GOT A WOK, MAKING A FRESH AND LIVELY DISH LIKE THIS ONE IS EASY. THE SALAD IS IDEAL FOR A LIGHT LUNCH ON A HOT AND LAZY SUMMER'S DAY. THE DRESSING IS DELICIOUS.

SERVES FOUR TO SIX

INGREDIENTS
4 skinless chicken breast fillets
2 garlic cloves, crushed
30ml/2 tbsp soy sauce
30ml/2 tbsp vegetable oil
115g/4oz/½ cup water
  chestnuts, sliced
50g/2oz/½ cup cashew nuts, roasted
  and coarsely chopped
4 shallots, thinly sliced
4 kaffir lime leaves, thinly sliced
1 lemon grass stalk, thinly sliced
5ml/1 tsp chopped fresh galangal
1 large fresh red chilli, seeded and
  finely chopped
2 spring onions (scallions),
  thinly sliced
10–12 fresh mint leaves, torn
1 lettuce, separated into leaves,
  to serve
2 fresh red chillies to garnish
For the dressing
120ml/4fl oz/½ cup coconut
  cream
30ml/2 tbsp Thai fish sauce
juice of 1 lime
30ml/2 tbsp palm sugar or light
  muscovado (brown) sugar

3 In a pan, heat the coconut cream, fish sauce, lime juice and sugar. Stir until the sugar has dissolved; set aside.

4 Tear the cooked chicken into strips and put it in a bowl. Add the water chestnuts, cashew nuts, shallots, kaffir lime leaves, lemon grass, galangal, red chilli, spring onions and mint leaves.

5 Pour the coconut dressing over the mixture and toss well. Serve the chicken on a bed of lettuce leaves and garnish with seeded and sliced red chillies.

1 Place the chicken in a large dish. Rub with the garlic and soy sauce and drizzle with 15ml/1 tbsp of the oil. Cover and marinate for 1–2 hours.

2 Heat the remaining oil in a wok or frying pan and stir-fry the chicken for 3–4 minutes on each side, or until cooked. Remove and set aside to cool.

Energy 216Kcal/905kJ; Protein 26.2g; Carbohydrate 7.8g, of which sugars 6.6g; Fat 9.1g, of which saturates 1.6g; Cholesterol 70mg; Calcium 23mg; Fibre 0.7g; Sodium 453mg.

LOTUS LEAF PARCELS FILLED WITH CHICKEN, RICE AND VEGETABLES

THE LOTUS LEAVES IMPART A DELICIOUS SMOKY FLAVOUR TO THE RICE IN THIS DISH. YOU CAN BUY THE DRIED LEAVES FROM ASIAN SUPERMARKETS. THE PARCELS MAKE A GREAT LUNCH OR SUPPER.

SERVES FOUR

INGREDIENTS
2 large lotus leaves
300g/11oz/1½ cups Thai jasmine
   rice
400ml/14fl oz/1⅔ cups vegetable
   or chicken stock
8 dried shiitake mushrooms
15ml/1 tbsp sunflower oil
200g/7oz skinless chicken thigh
   fillets, cut into small cubes
50g/2oz pancetta, cubed
3 garlic cloves, finely sliced
10ml/2 tsp finely grated
   fresh root ginger
50g/2oz carrots, cut into thin batons
50g/2oz mangetouts (snow peas),
   sliced down the middle
60ml/4 tbsp light soy sauce
15ml/1 tbsp Chinese rice wine
5ml/1 tsp cornflour (cornstarch)

1 Place the lotus leaves in a large bowl and pour over enough hot water to cover. Leave to soak for 1½ hours. Drain and cut in half, then set aside.

2 Place the rice in a wok and pour over the stock. Bring to the boil, then reduce the heat, cover and cook gently for 10 minutes. Remove from the heat.

3 Soak the mushrooms in boiling water for 15 minutes, drain, reserving the liquid. Squeeze them dry, discard the stems and thinly slice the caps.

4 Add the oil to a clean wok and place over a high heat. Add the chicken and pancetta and stir-fry for 2–3 minutes, until lightly browned. Add the garlic, ginger, carrots, mangetout and mushrooms and stir-fry for 30 seconds.

5 Add half the soy sauce, the rice wine and 60ml/4 tbsp of the reserved mushroom liquid to the wok.

6 Combine the cornflour with 15ml/1 tbsp cold water, add to the wok and cook for a few minutes until the mixture thickens. Add the rice and the remaining soy sauce and mix well.

7 Place the lotus leaves on a clean work surface (brown side down) and divide the chicken mixture among them. Fold in the sides of the leaves, then roll up and place the parcels, seam side down, in a baking parchment-lined bamboo steamer.

8 Cover the steamer and place over a wok of simmering water for about 20 minutes (replenishing the water in the wok if necessary). Serve the parcels immediately and unwrap at the table.

VARIATION
Use cooked broad (fava) beans instead of mangetouts, popping them out of their skins before adding to the wok.

Energy 377Kcal/1581kJ; Protein 20.7g; Carbohydrate 63.7g, of which sugars 2.4g; Fat 4g, of which saturates 1.2g; Cholesterol 43mg; Calcium 31mg; Fibre 0.8g; Sodium 1082mg.

SCENTED CHICKEN WRAPS

FOR SHEER SOPHISTICATION, THESE LEAF-WRAPPED CHICKEN BITES TAKE A LOT OF BEATING. THEY ARE SURPRISINGLY EASY TO MAKE AND CAN BE DEEP-FRIED IN MINUTES IN THE WOK.

SERVES FOUR

INGREDIENTS

    400g/14oz skinless chicken thighs,
      boned
    45ml/3 tbsp soy sauce
    30ml/2 tbsp finely grated garlic
    15ml/1 tbsp cumin
    15ml/1 tbsp ground coriander
    15ml/1 tbsp golden caster
      (superfine) sugar
    5ml/1 tsp finely grated fresh
      root ginger
    1 fresh bird's eye chilli
    30ml/2 tbsp oyster sauce
    15ml/1 tbsp Thai fish sauce
    1 bunch of pandanus leaves, to wrap
    vegetable oil, for deep-frying
    sweet chilli sauce, to serve

1 Using a cleaver or sharp knife, cut the chicken into bitesize pieces and place in a large mixing bowl.

2 Place the soy sauce, garlic, cumin, coriander, sugar, ginger, chilli, oyster sauce and fish sauce in a blender and process until smooth. Pour over the chicken, cover and leave to marinate in the refrigerator for 6-8 hours.

3 When ready to cook, drain the chicken from the marinade and wrap each piece in a pandanus leaf (you will need to cut the leaves to size) and secure with a cocktail stick (toothpick).

4 Fill a wok one-third full of oil and heat to 180°C/350°F or until a cube of bread, dropped into the oil, browns in 45 seconds. Carefully add the chicken parcels, 3–4 at a time, and deep-fry for 3–4 minutes, or until cooked through. Drain on kitchen paper and serve with the chilli sauce. (Do not eat the leaves!)

COOK'S TIP
Pandanus leaves are usually available from Asian supermarkets.

Energy 159Kcal/669kJ; Protein 24.5g; Carbohydrate 6.8g, of which sugars 6.6g; Fat 3.9g, of which saturates 0.6g; Cholesterol 70mg; Calcium 10mg; Fibre 0.1g; Sodium 1055mg.

THAI FRIED RICE

*THIS SUBSTANTIAL AND TASTY DISH IS BASED ON THAI JASMINE RICE COOKED IN COCONUT MILK.
DICED CHICKEN, RED PEPPER AND CORN KERNELS ADD COLOUR AND EXTRA FLAVOUR.*

SERVES FOUR

INGREDIENTS
  475ml/16fl oz/2 cups water
  50g/2oz/½ cup coconut milk powder
  350g/12oz/1¾ cups Thai jasmine
    rice, rinsed
  30ml/2 tbsp groundnut (peanut) oil
  2 garlic cloves, chopped
  1 small onion, finely chopped
  2.5cm/1in piece fresh root ginger,
    peeled and grated
  225g/8oz skinned chicken breast
    fillets, cut into 1cm/½in pieces
  1 red (bell) pepper, seeded
    and sliced
  115g/4oz/1 cup drained canned
    whole kernel corn
  5ml/1 tsp chilli oil
  5ml/1 tsp hot curry powder
  2 eggs, beaten
  salt
  spring onion (scallion) shreds,
    to garnish

1 Pour the water into a pan and whisk in the coconut milk powder. Add the rice and bring to the boil. Reduce the heat, cover and cook for 12 minutes, or until the rice is tender and the liquid has been absorbed. Spread the rice on a baking sheet and leave until cold.

2 Heat the oil in a wok, add the garlic, onion and ginger and stir-fry over a medium heat for 2 minutes.

COOK'S TIP
It is important that the rice is completely cold before being fried.

3 Push the onion mixture to the sides of the wok, add the chicken to the centre and stir-fry for 2 minutes. Add the rice and toss well. Stir-fry over a high heat for about 3 minutes more, until the chicken is cooked through.

4 Stir in the sliced red pepper, corn, chilli oil and curry powder, with salt to taste. Toss over the heat for 1 minute. Stir in the beaten eggs and cook for 1 minute more. Garnish with the spring onion shreds and serve.

Energy 563Kcal/2358kJ; Protein 26.7g; Carbohydrate 88.9g, of which sugars 13.9g; Fat 11.2g, of which saturates 2.1g; Cholesterol 139mg; Calcium 77mg; Fibre 1.8g; Sodium 284mg.

CHIANG MAI NOODLES

AN INTERESTING NOODLE DISH FROM THAILAND THAT COMBINES SOFT, BOILED NOODLES WITH CRISP
DEEP-FRIED ONES AND ADDS THE CLASSIC THAI CONTRAST OF SWEET, HOT AND SOUR FLAVOURS.

3 Add the chicken and toss over the heat until sealed on all sides. Stir in the soy sauce and the diced peppers and stir-fry for 3–4 minutes. Pour in the stock. Bring to the boil, then lower the heat and simmer for 10–15 minutes, until the chicken is fully cooked.

4 Meanwhile, make the noodle garnish. Heat the oil in a wok to 190°C/375°F or until a cube of bread, added to the oil, browns in 40 seconds. Break all the noodles in half, then divide them into four portions. Add one portion at a time to the hot oil. They will puff up on contact. As soon as they are crisp, lift the noodles out with a slotted spoon and drain on kitchen paper.

5 Bring a large pan of water to the boil and cook the fresh or dried noodles until tender, following the instructions on the packet. Drain well, divide among four warmed individual dishes, then spoon the curry sauce over them. Top each portion with a cluster of fried noodles. Sprinkle the chopped pickled garlic and coriander over the top and serve immediately, offering lime wedges for squeezing.

COOK'S TIP
Magic paste is a commercial product sold in jars in Asian stores. It is a blend of garlic, coriander (cilantro) root and white pepper. This combination of flavours is widely used in Thai home cooking. When mixed with red curry paste, magic paste gives a great flavour to this combination of chicken, red (bell) peppers and noodles.

SERVES FOUR

INGREDIENTS
  250ml/8fl oz/1 cup coconut cream
  15ml/1 tbsp magic paste
  5ml/1 tsp Thai red curry paste
  450g/1lb chicken thigh meat,
    chopped into small pieces
  30ml/2 tbsp dark soy sauce
  2 red (bell) peppers, seeded and
    finely diced
  600ml/1 pint/2½ cups chicken or
    vegetable stock
  90g/3½oz fresh or dried rice noodles
For the garnishes
  vegetable oil, for deep-frying
  90g/3½oz fine dried rice noodles
  2 pickled garlic cloves, chopped
  small bunch fresh coriander
    (cilantro), chopped
  2 limes, cut into wedges

1 Pour the coconut cream into a large wok and bring to the boil over a medium heat. Continue to boil, stirring frequently, for 8–10 minutes, until the milk separates and an oily sheen appears on the surface.

2 Add the magic paste and red curry paste and cook, stirring constantly, for 3–5 seconds, until fragrant.

Energy 245Kcal/1034kJ; Protein 29.4g; Carbohydrate 27.6g, of which sugars 9g; Fat 1.8g, of which saturates 0.6g; Cholesterol 79mg; Calcium 35mg; Fibre 1.4g; Sodium 677mg.

ORANGE AND GINGER GLAZED POUSSINS

THESE MOIST, SUCCULENT POUSSINS COATED IN A SPICED CITRUS AND HONEY GLAZE MAKE A GREAT ALTERNATIVE TO A TRADITIONAL ROAST. BE SURE TO PLAN AHEAD BECAUSE THEY NEED TO BE MARINATED FOR AT LEAST 6 HOURS, BEFORE BEING COOKED IN THE WOK.

SERVES FOUR

INGREDIENTS

- 4 poussins, 300–350g/11–12oz each
- juice and finely grated rind of 2 oranges
- 2 garlic cloves, crushed
- 15ml/1 tbsp grated fresh root ginger
- 90ml/6 tbsp soy sauce
- 75ml/5 tbsp clear honey
- 2–3 star anise
- 30ml/2 tbsp Chinese rice wine
- about 20 kaffir lime leaves
- a large bunch of spring onions (scallions), shredded
- 60ml/4 tbsp butter
- 1 large orange, segmented

1 Place the poussins in a deep, non-metallic dish. Combine the orange rind and juice, garlic, ginger, half the soy sauce, half the honey, star anise and rice wine, then pour the mixture over the poussins. Turn the poussins so they are coated all over in the marinade. Cover the dish with clear film (plastic wrap), and place in the refrigerator for at least 6 hours to marinate.

2 To cook the poussins, line a large, heatproof plate with the kaffir lime leaves and spring onions. Lift the poussins out of the marinade and place on top of the layer of leaves. Reserve the marinade in a jug (pitcher).

3 Place a trivet or steamer rack in the base of a large wok and pour in 5cm/2in water. Bring to the boil and carefully lower the plate of poussins on to the trivet or rack. Cover, reduce the heat to low and steam for 45 minutes–1 hour, or until the poussins are cooked through and tender. (Check the water level regularly and add more when necessary.)

4 Remove the poussins from the wok and keep warm while you make the glaze. Wipe out the wok and pour in the reserved marinade, butter and the remaining soy sauce and honey. Bring to the boil, reduce the heat and cook gently for 10–15 minutes, or until thick.

5 Spoon the glaze over the poussins and serve immediately, garnished with the orange segments.

COOK'S TIP
You can make easily make this for fewer people. Just use one poussin and reduce the amount of glaze accordingly. A single bird can be cooked in a steamer basket wrapped with banana leaves.

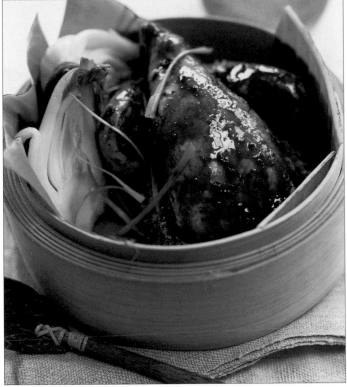

Energy 568Kcal/2378kJ; Protein 67.3g; Carbohydrate 18.7g, of which sugars 18.5g; Fat 25.3g, of which saturates 11.1g; Cholesterol 32mg; Calcium 110mg; Fibre 0.7g; Sodium 1344mg.

SHREDDED DUCK AND NOODLE SALAD

THIS REFRESHING, PIQUANT SALAD MAKES A MOUTHWATERING FIRST COURSE OR LIGHT MEAL. THE MARINATED DUCK IS LOVELY AND MOIST, HAVING BEEN STEAMED IN THE WOK, AND TASTES SUPERB WITH THE FRESH RAW VEGETABLES, NOODLES AND ZESTY DRESSING.

SERVES FOUR

INGREDIENTS

4 duck breast portions
30ml/2 tbsp Chinese rice wine
10ml/2 tsp finely grated fresh
  root ginger
60ml/4 tbsp soy sauce
15ml/1 tbsp sesame oil
15ml/1 tbsp clear honey
10ml/2 tsp Chinese five-spice powder
toasted sesame seeds, to sprinkle
For the noodles
150g/5oz bean-thread noodles
a small handful of fresh mint leaves
a small handful of coriander
  (cilantro) leaves
1 red (bell) pepper, seeded and
  finely sliced
4 spring onions (scallions), finely
  shredded or sliced
50g/2oz mixed salad leaves
For the dressing
45ml/3 tbsp light soy sauce
30ml/2 tbsp mirin
10ml/2 tsp golden caster
  (superfine) sugar
1 garlic clove, crushed
10ml/2 tsp chilli oil

1 Place the duck breast portions in a non-metallic bowl. Mix together the rice wine, ginger, soy sauce, sesame oil, clear honey and five-spice powder. Toss to coat, cover and marinate in the refrigerator for 3–4 hours.

VARIATIONS
If you prefer, you can use shredded chicken in place of the duck.

2 Double over a large sheet of heavy foil. Place the foil on a heatproof plate. Place the duck breast portions on it and spoon the marinade over. Fold the foil to enclose the duck and juices and scrunch the edges to seal.

3 Place a trivet or steamer rack in a large wok and pour in water to a depth of about 5cm/2in. Bring to the boil and place the plate on to the trivet or rack. Cover tightly, reduce the heat and steam gently for 50–60 minutes. Remove the plate from the wok and leave to rest for 15 minutes.

4 Place the noodles in a large bowl and pour over boiling water to cover. Cover and soak for 5–6 minutes. Drain, refresh under cold water and drain again. Put in a bowl with the herbs, red pepper, spring onions and salad leaves.

5 Mix together all the dressing ingredients. Remove the skin from the duck breasts and roughly shred the flesh using a fork. Divide the noodle salad among four plates and top with the shredded duck. Spoon over the dressing, sprinkle with the sesame seeds and serve immediately.

Energy 398Kcal/1671kJ; Protein 32.8g; Carbohydrate 41.7g, of which sugars 10.8g; Fat 11.6g, of which saturates 2.2g; Cholesterol 165mg; Calcium 40mg; Fibre 1g; Sodium 1688mg.

DUCK AND SESAME STIR-FRY

THIS RECIPE COMES FROM NORTHERN THAILAND AND IS INTENDED FOR GAME BIRDS, AS FARMED DUCK WOULD HAVE TOO MUCH FAT. USE WILD DUCK IF YOU CAN GET IT, OR EVEN PARTRIDGE, PHEASANT OR PIGEON. IF YOU DO USE FARMED DUCK, YOU SHOULD REMOVE THE SKIN AND FAT LAYER.

SERVES FOUR

INGREDIENTS
250g/9oz boneless wild duck meat
15ml/1 tbsp sesame oil
15ml/1 tbsp vegetable oil
4 garlic cloves, finely sliced
2.5ml/½ tsp dried chilli flakes
15ml/1 tbsp Thai fish sauce
15ml/1 tbsp light soy sauce
120ml/4fl oz/½ cup water
1 head broccoli, cut into small florets
coriander (cilantro) and 15ml/1 tbsp
toasted sesame seeds, to garnish

VARIATIONS
Pak choi (bok choy) or Chinese flowering cabbage can be used instead of broccoli.

1 Cut the duck meat into bitesize pieces. Heat the wok, add the oils and, when hot, stir-fry the garlic over a medium heat until it is golden brown – do not let it burn. Add the duck to the pan and stir-fry for a further 2 minutes, until the meat begins to brown.

2 Stir in the chilli flakes, fish sauce, soy sauce and water. Add the broccoli and continue to stir-fry for about 2 minutes, until the duck is just cooked through.

3 Serve on warmed plates, garnished with coriander and sesame seeds.

Energy 192Kcal/798kJ; Protein 18.7g; Carbohydrate 2.7g, of which sugars 2.3g; Fat 12.9g, of which saturates 2.1g; Cholesterol 69mg; Calcium 104mg; Fibre 3.6g; Sodium 436mg.

BEEF RENDANG

IN INDONESIA, WHERE THIS SPICY DISH ORIGINATED, IT IS USUALLY SERVED WITH THE MEAT QUITE DRY; IF YOU PREFER MORE SAUCE, SIMPLY ADD MORE WATER WHEN STIRRING IN THE POTATOES. THE DEEP FRIED ONIONS, TRADITIONALLY SERVED WITH THE BEEF, ADD A DELICIOUS, CRISPY CONTRAST.

SERVES SIX–EIGHT

INGREDIENTS
2 onions or 5–6 shallots, chopped
4 garlic cloves, chopped
2.5cm/1in piece fresh galangal,
  peeled and sliced, or 15ml/1 tbsp
  galangal paste
2.5cm/1in piece fresh root ginger,
  peeled and sliced
4–6 fresh red chillies, seeded
  and roughly chopped
lower part only of 1 lemon grass
  stem, sliced
2.5cm/1in piece fresh turmeric,
  peeled and sliced, or 5ml/1 tsp
  ground turmeric
1kg/2¼lb prime beef in one piece
5ml/1 tsp coriander seeds,
  dry-fried
5ml/1 tsp cumin seeds, dry-fried
2 kaffir lime leaves, torn into
  pieces
2 x 400ml/14fl oz cans coconut
  milk
300ml/½ pint/1¼ cups water
30ml/2 tbsp dark soy sauce
5ml/1 tsp tamarind pulp, soaked in
  60ml/4 tbsp warm water
8–10 small new potatoes, well
  scrubbed and eyed
salt and ground black pepper
deep-fried onions (see below),
  sliced fresh red chillies and spring
  onions (scallions), to garnish

1 Put the onions or shallots in a food processor. Add the garlic, galangal, ginger, chillies, sliced lemon grass and fresh or ground turmeric. Process to a fine paste or grind in a mortar, using a pestle.

2 Cut the meat into cubes using a large sharp knife, then place the cubes in a bowl.

3 Grind the dry-fried coriander and cumin seeds, then add to the meat with the onion, chilli paste and kaffir lime leaves; stir well. Cover and leave in a cool place to marinate while you prepare the other ingredients.

COOK'S TIP
This dish is even better if you can cook it a day or two in advance of serving, which allows the flavours to mellow beautifully. Add the potatoes on reheating and simmer until tender.

4 Pour the coconut milk and water into a wok, then stir in the spiced meat and the soy sauce. Strain the tamarind water and add to the wok. Stir over medium heat until the liquid boils, then simmer gently, half-covered, for 1½ hours.

5 Add the potatoes and simmer for 20–25 minutes, or until the meat and the potatoes are tender. Add water if you prefer. Season and serve, garnished with the deep-fried onions, chillies and spring onions.

DEEP-FRIED ONIONS

KNOWN AS BAWANG GORENG, THESE ARE A TRADITIONAL GARNISH AND ACCOMPANY MANY INDONESIAN DISHES. ASIAN STORES SELL THEM READY-PREPARED, BUT IT IS EASY TO MAKE THEM. THE SMALL RED ONIONS SOLD IN ASIAN STORES ARE EXCELLENT BECAUSE THEY CONTAIN LESS WATER.

MAKES 450G/1LB

INGREDIENTS
450g/1lb onions
vegetable oil, for deep-frying

1 Thinly slice the onions with a sharp knife or in a food processor. Spread the slices out in a single layer on several sheets of kitchen paper and leave them to dry, in an airy place, for no less than 30 minutes and up to 2 hours.

2 Heat the oil in a wok to 190°C/375°F. Fry the onions in batches, until crisp and golden, turning all the time. Drain well on kitchen paper, cool and store in an airtight container, unless you are using them immediately.

Energy 289Kcal/1210kJ; Protein 30.2g; Carbohydrate 15.4g, of which sugars 8.6g; Fat 12.2g, of which saturates 5g; Cholesterol 73mg; Calcium 63mg; Fibre 1.4g; Sodium 465mg.
For 450g: Energy 854Kcal/3521kJ; Protein 5.4g; Carbohydrate 35.5g, of which sugars 25.2g; Fat 77.8g, of which saturates 9g; Cholesterol 0mg; Calcium 113mg; Fibre 6.3g; Sodium 14mg.

SPICY MEAT BALLS

A WOK IS GREAT FOR COOKING MEAT BALLS BECAUSE YOU CAN PUSH THE COOKED ONES UP THE SIDES.
CHILLI SAMBAL IS FIERCELY HOT, SO BE CAREFUL HOW MUCH YOU ADD TO YOUR MOUTHFUL.

SERVES FOUR TO SIX

INGREDIENTS
  1cm/¹/₂in cube shrimp paste
  1 large onion, roughly chopped
  1–2 fresh red chillies, seeded
    and chopped
  2 garlic cloves, crushed
  15ml/1 tbsp coriander seeds
  5ml/1 tsp cumin seeds
  450g/1lb lean minced (ground) beef
  10ml/2 tsp dark soy sauce
  5ml/1 tsp dark brown sugar
  juice of 1¹/₂ lemons
  a little beaten egg
  vegetable oil, for shallow frying
  salt and ground black pepper
  1 green and 2 fresh red chillies,
    to garnish
  Chilli Sambal, to serve

1 Wrap the shrimp paste in a piece of foil and warm in a frying pan for 5 minutes, turning a few times. Unwrap and put in a food processor.

COOK'S TIP
When processing the shrimp paste (blachan), onion, chillies and garlic, do not process for too long, otherwise the onion will become too wet and spoil the consistency of the meat balls.

2 Add the onion, chillies and garlic to the food processor and process until finely chopped. Set aside. Dry fry the coriander and cumin seeds in a hot frying pan for 1 minute, to release the aroma. Place the seeds in a mortar and grind with a pestle.

3 Put the meat in a large bowl. Stir in the onion mixture. Add the ground spices, soy sauce, brown sugar, lemon juice and beaten egg. Season to taste.

4 Shape the meat mixture into small, even-size balls, and chill these for 5–10 minutes to firm them up.

5 Heat the oil in a wok or large frying pan and fry the meat balls for 4–5 minutes, turning often, until cooked through and browned. You may have to do this in batches.

6 Drain the meat balls on kitchen paper, and then pile them on to a warm serving platter or into a large serving bowl. Finely slice the green chilli and one of the red chillies and scatter over the meat balls. Garnish with the remaining red chilli, if you like. Serve with the Chilli Sambal (see below) handed round separately.

VARIATION
Minced beef is traditionally used for this dish, but minced pork, lamb – or even turkey – would also be good.

CHILLI SAMBAL

THIS FIERCE CONDIMENT IS BOTTLED AS SAMBAL OELEK, BUT IT IS EASY TO PREPARE AND WILL KEEP
FOR SEVERAL WEEKS IN A WELL-SEALED JAR IN THE REFRIGERATOR. USE A STAINLESS-STEEL OR PLASTIC
SPOON TO MEASURE; IF SAUCE DRIPS ON YOUR FINGERS, WASH WELL IN SOAPY WATER IMMEDIATELY.

MAKES 450G/1LB

INGREDIENTS
  450g/1lb fresh red chillies, seeded
  10ml/2 tsp salt

1 Bring a saucepan of water to the boil, add the seeded chillies and cook them for 5–8 minutes.

2 Drain the chillies and then grind them in a food processor, without making the paste too smooth. Stir in the salt.

3 Spoon into small individual dishes, to serve with the Spicy Meat Balls. Alternatively, transfer to a screw-topped glass jar, and cover with a piece of greaseproof (waxed) paper. Screw on the lid and store in the refrigerator for up to 3 weeks.

Energy 255Kcal/1057kJ; Protein 15.8g; Carbohydrate 4.1g, of which sugars 3.2g; Fat 19.6g, of which saturates 6.1g; Cholesterol 49mg; Calcium 28mg; Fibre 0.6g; Sodium 216mg.
For 450g: Energy 90Kcal/374kJ; Protein 13.1g; Carbohydrate 3.1g, of which sugars 3.1g; Fat 2.7g, of which saturates 0g; Cholesterol 0mg; Calcium 136mg; Fibre 0g; Sodium 3962mg.

PORK CHOPS <u>WITH</u> FIELD MUSHROOMS

EVEN THOUGH THE PORK CHOPS AND MUSHROOMS ARE COOKED ON THE BARBECUE OR GRIDDLE, THE WOK IS USED FOR MAKING THE QUICK, EASY SAUCE THAT IS SPOONED OVER THEM. SERVE THE PORK AND MUSHROOMS OVER NOODLES OR WITH THAI JASMINE RICE.

SERVES FOUR

INGREDIENTS
    4 pork chops
    4 large field (portabello) mushrooms
    45ml/3 tbsp vegetable oil
    4 fresh red chillies, seeded and
        thinly sliced
    45ml/3 tbsp Thai fish sauce
    90ml/6 tbsp fresh lime juice
    4 shallots, chopped
    5ml/1 tsp roasted ground rice
    30ml/2 tbsp spring onions
        (scallions), chopped, plus shredded
        spring onions to garnish
    coriander (cilantro) leaves, to garnish
For the marinade
    2 garlic cloves, chopped
    15ml/1 tbsp granulated sugar
    15ml/1 tbsp Thai fish sauce
    30ml/2 tbsp soy sauce
    15ml/1 tbsp sesame oil
    15ml/1 tbsp whisky or dry sherry
    2 lemon grass stalks, finely chopped
    2 spring onions (scallions), chopped

1 Make the marinade. Combine the garlic, sugar, sauces, oil and whisky or sherry in a large, shallow dish. Stir in the lemon grass and spring onions.

2 Add the pork chops, turning to coat them in the marinade. Cover and leave to marinate for 1–2 hours.

3 Lift the chops out of the marinade and place them on a barbecue grid over hot coals or on a grill (broiler) rack. Add the mushrooms and brush them with 15ml/1 tbsp of the oil. Cook the pork chops for 5–7 minutes on each side and the mushrooms for about 2 minutes. Brush both with the marinade while cooking.

4 Heat the remaining oil in a wok or small frying pan, then remove the pan from the heat and stir in the chillies, fish sauce, lime juice, shallots, ground rice and chopped spring onions. Put the pork chops and mushrooms on a large serving plate and spoon over the sauce. Garnish with the coriander leaves and shredded spring onion.

Energy 293Kcal/1229kJ; Protein 44.4g; Carbohydrate 2.9g, of which sugars 1.4g; Fat 11.1g, of which saturates 3.3g; Cholesterol 126mg; Calcium 24mg; Fibre 0.9g; Sodium 411mg.

SWEET AND SOUR PORK

THIS CLASSIC CHINESE-STYLE DISH, WITH ITS STUNNING COLOURS, PIQUANT SWEET AND SOUR SAUCE AND GLORIOUSLY STICKY TEXTURE, MAKES A TASTY SUPPER. SERVE WITH FRIED RICE AND STEAMED ASIAN GREENS TO CREATE AN AUTHENTIC CHINESE MEAL.

SERVES FOUR

INGREDIENTS

1 carrot
1 red (bell) pepper
4 spring onions (scallions)
45ml/3 tbsp light soy sauce
15ml/1 tbsp Chinese rice wine
15ml/1 tbsp sesame oil
5ml/1 tsp freshly ground
   black pepper
500g/1¼lb pork loin, cut into
   1cm/½in cubes
65g/2½oz/9 tbsp cornflour
   (cornstarch)
65g/2½oz/9 tbsp plain
   (all-purpose) flour
5ml/1 tsp bicarbonate of soda
   (baking soda)
sunflower oil, for deep-frying
10ml/2 tsp finely grated garlic
5ml/1 tsp finely grated fresh
   root ginger
60ml/4 tbsp tomato ketchup
30ml/2 tbsp caster (superfine) sugar
15ml/1 tbsp rice vinegar
15ml/1 tbsp cornflour (cornstarch)
   blended with 120ml/4fl oz/
   ½ cup water
egg fried rice or noodles, to serve
salt

2 In a large mixing bowl, combine 15ml/1 tbsp of the soy sauce with the rice wine, sesame oil and pepper. Add the pork and toss to mix. Cover and chill for 3–4 hours.

4 Fill a wok one-third full with the sunflower oil and heat to 180°C/350°F or until a cube of bread browns in 45 seconds. Separate the pork cubes and deep-fry them, in batches, for 1–2 minutes, or until golden. Remove and drain on kitchen paper.

5 Mix together the garlic, ginger, tomato ketchup, sugar, the remaining soy sauce, rice vinegar and cornflour mixture. Place a small pan over a medium heat. Add the mixture and heat for 2–3 minutes, until thickened. Add the carrot, red pepper and spring onions, stir and remove from the heat.

1 Using a sharp knife or cleaver, chop the carrots in half, then in slices, and then into thin shreds. Cut the pepper into sections and shred into similar sized pieces. Cut the spring onions in half, then cut each half into shreds.

3 Combine the cornflour, plain flour and bicarbonate of soda in a bowl. Add a pinch of salt and mix in 150ml/¼ pint/ ⅔ cup cold water to make a thick batter. Add the pork to the batter and mix well with your hands to coat evenly.

6 Reheat the deep-frying oil in the wok to 180°C/350°F and then re-fry the pork pieces in batches for 1–2 minutes, until golden and crisp. Drain and add to the sauce and toss to mix well. Serve with egg fried rice or noodles.

Energy 445Kcal/1873kJ; Protein 29.8g; Carbohydrate 52.2g, of which sugars 17.4g; Fat 13.9g, of which saturates 2.9g; Cholesterol 79mg; Calcium 55mg; Fibre 2g; Sodium 1154mg.

PAN-FRIED PORK WITH GINGER SAUCE

REPUTEDLY CREATED BY A CANTEEN DINNER LADY AT A TOKYO UNIVERSITY DURING THE 1970S, THIS DISH, KNOWN AS BUTA-NIKU SHOGA YAKI, IS PARTICULARLY POPULAR WITH YOUNGSTERS.

SERVES FOUR

INGREDIENTS
  450g/1lb pork chops, boned
    and trimmed
  15ml/1 tbsp vegetable oil
  1 small onion, thinly sliced
    lengthways
  50g/2oz/1 cup beansprouts
  50g/2oz mangetouts (snow peas),
    trimmed
  salt
For the marinade
  15ml/1 tbsp shoyu
  15ml/1 tbsp sake
  15ml/1 tbsp mirin
  4cm/1½in piece fresh root ginger,
    very finely grated,
    plus juice

1 Wrap the pork chops in clear film (plastic wrap) and freeze for 2 hours. Cut into 3mm/⅛in slices, then into 4cm/1½in wide strips.

2 To make the marinade, mix all the ingredients in a plastic container. Add the pork and marinate for 15 minutes.

3 Heat the vegetable oil in a wok on a medium-high heat. Add the onion and stir-fry for 3 minutes.

4 Take half of the pork slices out of the marinade and add to the wok. Transfer the meat to a plate when its colour changes; this will take only about 2–3 minutes. Repeat the process with the rest of the meat and reserve the marinade. Transfer all the cooked pork slices and onions to the plate.

5 Pour the reserved marinade into the wok and simmer until it has reduced by one-third. Add the beansprouts and mangetouts, then the pork and increase the heat to medium-high for 2 minutes.

6 Heap the beansprouts on individual serving plates and lean the meat, onions and mangetouts against them. Serve immediately.

DEEP-FRIED PORK FILLET

THIS INVIGORATING JAPANESE DISH IS SO GOOD THAT SOME RESTAURANTS SERVE NOTHING ELSE. THE PORK IS ALWAYS GARNISHED WITH A HEAP OF VERY FINELY SHREDDED WHITE CABBAGE.

SERVES FOUR

INGREDIENTS
  1 white cabbage
  4 pork loin chops or cutlets, boned
  plain (all-purpose) flour, to dust
  vegetable oil, for deep-frying
  2 eggs, beaten
  50g/2oz/1 cup dried
    white breadcrumbs
  salt and ready-ground mixed pepper
  prepared English (hot) mustard,
    to garnish
  Japanese pickles, to serve
For the sauce
  60ml/4 tbsp Worcestershire sauce
  30ml/2 tbsp good-quality
    tomato ketchup
  5ml/1 tsp shoyu

1 Quarter the cabbage and remove the central core. Slice the wedges very finely with a vegetable slicer or a sharp knife.

2 Make a few deep cuts horizontally across the fat of the meat. This prevents the meat curling up while cooking. Rub a little salt and pepper into the meat and dust with the flour, then shake off any excess.

3 Heat the oil to 180°C/350°F, or until a cube of bread browns in 45 seconds.

4 Dip the meat in the beaten eggs, then coat with breadcrumbs. Deep-fry two pieces at a time for 8–10 minutes, or until golden brown. Drain on a wire rack or on kitchen paper. Repeat until all the pieces of pork are deep-fried.

5 Heap the cabbage on four individual serving plates. Cut the pork crossways into 2cm/¾in thick strips and arrange them to your liking on the cabbage.

6 To make the *ton-katsu* sauce, mix the Worcestershire sauce, ketchup and shoyu in a jug (pitcher) or gravy boat. Serve the pork and cabbage immediately, with the sauce, mustard and Japanese pickles. Pickles can also be served in separate dishes, if you like.

Energy 179Kcal/747kJ; Protein 25.3g; Carbohydrate 2.8g, of which sugars 2.1g; Fat 7.4g, of which saturates 1.9g; Cholesterol 71mg; Calcium 21mg; Fibre 0.7g; Sodium 614mg.
Energy 311Kcal/1304kJ; Protein 31.1g; Carbohydrate 21.7g, of which sugars 12g; Fat 11.6g, of which saturates 2.9g; Cholesterol 166mg; Calcium 141mg; Fibre 3.5g; Sodium 522mg.

POPIAH

THIS IS THE STRAITS CHINESE OR NONYA VERSION OF THE SPRING ROLL. DO NOT BE PUT OFF BY THE NUMBER OF INGREDIENTS; IT TAKES A LITTLE TIME TO GET EVERYTHING TOGETHER BUT ONCE IT IS ALL ON THE TABLE THE COOK CAN RELAX AS GUESTS ASSEMBLE THEIR OWN ROLLS.

MAKES ABOUT TWENTY PANCAKES

INGREDIENTS
40g/1¹/₂oz/¹/₃ cup cornflour
  (cornstarch)
215g/7¹/₂oz/generous 1³/₄ cups
  plain (all-purpose) flour
salt
450ml/³/₄ pint/scant 2 cups water
6 eggs, beaten
lard (white cooking fat), for frying
For the cooked filling
30ml/2 tbsp vegetable oil
1 onion, finely chopped
2 garlic cloves, crushed
115g/4oz cooked pork, chopped
115g/4oz crab meat or peeled cooked
  prawns (shrimp), thawed if frozen
115g/4oz drained canned bamboo
  shoot, thinly sliced
1 small yam bean, peeled and grated,
  or 12 drained canned water
  chestnuts, finely chopped
15–30ml/1–2 tbsp yellow
  salted beans
15ml/1 tbsp light soy sauce
ground black pepper
For the fresh fillings
2 hard-boiled eggs, chopped
2 Chinese sausages, steamed
  and sliced
115g/4oz packet fried tofu, each
  piece halved
225g/8oz/4 cups beansprouts
115g/4oz crab meat or peeled
  cooked prawns (shrimp)
¹/₂ cucumber, cut into matchsticks
small bunch of spring onions
  (scallions), finely chopped
20 lettuce leaves, rinsed and dried
fresh coriander (cilantro) sprigs, to
  garnish
selection of sauces, including bottled
  chopped chillies, bottled chopped
  garlic and hoisin sauce, to serve

COOK'S TIP
Yam beans are not beans at all, but large tubers with a mild sweet flavour, and a texture similar to water chestnuts.

1 Sift the flours and salt into a bowl. Add the measured water and eggs and mix to a smooth batter.

2 Grease a heavy-based frying pan with lard. Heat the pan, pouring off any excess lard, then pour in just enough batter to cover the base.

3 As soon as it sets, flip and cook the other side. The pancakes should be quite thin. Repeat with the remaining batter to make 20–24 pancakes in all. Pile the cooked pancakes on top of each other, with a layer of baking parchment between each to prevent them sticking. Wrap in foil and keep warm in a low oven.

4 Make the cooked filling. Heat the oil in a wok and stir-fry the onion and garlic for 5 minutes until softened but not browned.

5 Add the pork, crab meat or prawns, bamboo shoot and grated yam bean or water chestnuts. Stir-fry the mixture over a medium heat for 2–3 minutes.

6 Add the salted yellow beans and soy sauce to the wok, with pepper to taste. Cover and cook gently for 15–20 minutes, adding a little water if the mixture starts to dry out. Spoon into a serving bowl and allow to cool.

7 Meanwhile, arrange the chopped hard-boiled eggs, sliced Chinese sausages, sliced tofu, beansprouts, crab meat or prawns, cucumber, spring onions and lettuce leaves in piles on a large platter or in separate bowls. Spoon the bottled chopped chillies, bottled chopped garlic and hoisin sauce into small bowls.

8 Each person makes up his or her own popiah by spreading a very small amount of chopped chilli, garlic or hoisin sauce on a pancake, adding a lettuce leaf, a little of the cooked filling and a small selection of the fresh ingredients. The pancake wrapper should not be over-filled.

9 The ends can be tucked in and the pancake rolled up in typical spring roll fashion, then eaten in the hand. They also look attractive simply rolled with the filling showing.

VARIATION
The popiah can be filled and rolled before guests arrive, in which case, garnish with sprigs of coriander. It is more fun though for everyone to fill and roll their own.

Energy 141Kcal/592kJ; Protein 9.2g; Carbohydrate 10.9g, of which sugars 1.3g; Fat 7.1g, of which saturates 1.2g; Cholesterol 89mg; Calcium 162mg; Fibre 0.8g; Sodium 181mg.

WARM LAMB AND NOODLE SALAD WITH MINT

THIS THAI-INSPIRED SALAD COMBINES THIN SLICES OF WOK-FRIED LAMB WITH LIGHTLY COOKED FRESH VEGETABLES AND RICE NOODLES, ALL TOSSED TOGETHER WITH A DELICIOUSLY FRAGRANT, AROMATIC, ASIAN-STYLE DRESSING, THEN HEAPED ARTISTICALLY ON INDIVIDUAL PLATES.

SERVES FOUR

INGREDIENTS
- 30ml/2 tbsp red Thai curry paste
- 60ml/4 tbsp sunflower oil
- 750g/1lb 11oz lamb neck fillets, thinly sliced
- 250g/9oz sugar snap peas
- 500g/1¼lb fresh rice noodles
- 1 red (bell) pepper, seeded and very thinly sliced
- 1 cucumber, cut into very thin slices with a vegetable peeler
- 6–7 spring onions (scallions), sliced diagonally
- a large handful of fresh mint leaves

For the dressing
- 15ml/1 tbsp sunflower oil
- juice of 2 limes
- 1 garlic clove, crushed
- 15ml/1 tbsp sugar
- 15ml/1 tbsp Thai fish sauce
- 30ml/2 tbsp soy sauce

1 In a shallow dish, mix together the red curry paste and half the oil. Add the lamb slices and toss to coat. Cover and leave to marinate in the refrigerator for up to 24 hours.

2 Blanch the sugar snap peas in a wok of lightly salted boiling water for 1–2 minutes. Drain, refresh under cold water, drain again thoroughly and transfer to a large bowl.

3 Put the noodles in a separate bowl and pour over boiling water to cover. Leave to soak for 5–10 minutes, until tender, then drain well and separate into strands with your fingers.

4 Add the noodles to the bowl containing the sugar snap peas, then add the sliced red pepper, cucumber and spring onions. Toss lightly to mix.

5 Heat a wok over a high heat and add the remaining sunflower oil. Stir-fry the lamb, in two batches, for 3–4 minutes, or until cooked through, then add to the bowl of salad ingredients.

6 Place all the dressing ingredients in a screw-top jar, screw on the lid and shake well to combine. Pour the dressing over the warm salad, sprinkle over the fresh mint leaves and toss well to combine. Serve immediately.

Energy 820Kcal/3418kJ; Protein 46g; Carbohydrate 76.4g, of which sugars 9.4g; Fat 36g, of which saturates 11.7g; Cholesterol 143mg; Calcium 55mg; Fibre 4.1g; Sodium 709mg.

COCONUT SPICED LAMB ᴼᴺ POPPADUMS

CRISP, MELT-IN-THE-MOUTH MINI POPPADUMS MAKE A GREAT BASE FOR THESE DIVINE LITTLE BITES.
TOP THEM WITH A DRIZZLE OF YOGURT AND A SPOONFUL OF MANGO CHUTNEY, THEN SERVE
IMMEDIATELY. TO MAKE AN EQUALLY TASTY VARIATION, USE CHICKEN OR PORK IN PLACE OF THE LAMB.

MAKES TWENTY-FIVE

INGREDIENTS
    30ml/2 tbsp sunflower oil
    4 shallots, finely chopped
    30ml/2 tbsp medium curry paste
    300g/11oz minced (ground) lamb
    90ml/6 tbsp tomato purée (paste)
    5ml/1 tsp caster (superfine) sugar
    200ml/7fl oz/scant 1 cup
       coconut cream
    juice of 1 lime
    60ml/4 tbsp chopped fresh
       mint leaves
    vegetable oil, for deep-frying
    salt and ground black pepper
    25 mini poppadums
    natural (plain) yogurt and
       mango chutney, to drizzle
    1 red chilli cut into slivers and mint
       leaves, to garnish

1 Heat the oil in a wok over a medium heat and stir-fry the shallots for 4–5 minutes, then add the curry paste. Stir-fry for 1 minute and then add the lamb. Stir-fry over a high heat for a further 4–5 minutes, then stir in the tomato purée, sugar and coconut cream.

2 Simmer the lamb for 25–30 minutes, until the liquid has been reduced. Season and stir in the lime juice and mint. Turn off the heat and keep warm.

3 Fill a separate wok one-third full of oil and heat to 180°C/350°F or until a cube of bread browns in 40 seconds. Deep-fry the poppadums for 30–40 seconds. Drain on kitchen paper.

4 Place the poppadums on a serving platter. Put a spoonful of spiced lamb on each one, then top with a little yogurt and mango chutney. Serve immediately, garnished with slivers of red chilli and mint leaves.

Energy 63Kcal/260kJ; Protein 2.7g; Carbohydrate 2.7g, of which sugars 1.3g; Fat 4.7g, of which saturates 1.4g; Cholesterol 9mg; Calcium 7mg; Fibre 0.3g; Sodium 45mg.

FISH AND SHELLFISH

Some of the finest recipes for the wok feature shellfish and fish, and no wonder, for steaming, stir-frying and deep-frying are perfect methods for cooking these ingredients. Whether your taste is for a rich fish curry, or for something with a crisp and crunchy coating, such as Deep-fried Skate Wings with Wasabi, or the sumptuous Langoustines with Lemon Grass Risotto, the wok will prove to be the perfect utensil. If your wok will accommodate a large steamer, you can even steam fish whole, wrapped in banana leaves to seal in the superb flavours. For smaller portions of fish, use a regular steamer, or a stack, which will allow you to steam vegetables at the same time.

SATAY PRAWNS

THIS DELICIOUS DISH IS INSPIRED BY THE CLASSIC INDONESIAN SATAY. THE COMBINATION OF MILD PEANUTS, AROMATIC SPICES, SWEET COCONUT MILK AND ZESTY LEMON JUICE IN THE SPICY DIP IS PERFECT AND IS GUARANTEED TO HAVE GUESTS COMING BACK FOR MORE.

SERVES FOUR TO SIX

INGREDIENTS
  450g/1lb king prawns (jumbo shrimp)
  25ml/1½ tbsp vegetable oil
For the peanut sauce
  25ml/1½ tbsp vegetable oil
  15ml/1 tbsp chopped garlic
  1 small onion, chopped
  3–4 fresh red chillies, seeded
    and chopped
  3 kaffir lime leaves, torn
  1 lemon grass stalk, bruised
    and chopped
  5ml/1 tsp medium curry paste
  250ml/8fl oz/1 cup coconut milk
  1cm/½in piece cinnamon stick
  75g/3oz/⅓ cup crunchy
    peanut butter
  45ml/3 tbsp tamarind juice, made
    by mixing tamarind paste with
    warm water
  30ml/2 tbsp Thai fish sauce
  30ml/2 tbsp palm sugar or light
    muscovado (brown) sugar
  juice of ½ lemon
For the garnish
  spring onions (scallions),
    cut diagonally
  ½ bunch fresh coriander
    (cilantro) leaves (optional)
  4 fresh red chillies, finely sliced
    (optional)

1 Remove the heads from the prawns and peel, leaving the tail ends intact. Slit each prawn along the back with a small, sharp knife and remove the black vein. Rinse under cold running water, pat completely dry on kitchen paper and set the prawns aside.

2 Make the peanut sauce. Heat half the oil in a wok or large, heavy frying pan. Add the garlic and onion and cook over a medium heat, stirring occasionally, for 3–4 minutes, until the mixture has softened but not browned.

3 Add the chillies, kaffir lime leaves, lemon grass and curry paste. Stir well and cook for a further 2–3 minutes, then stir in the coconut milk, cinnamon stick, peanut butter, tamarind juice, fish sauce, sugar and lemon juice. Cook, stirring constantly, until well blended.

4 Bring to the boil, then reduce the heat to low and simmer gently for 15–20 minutes, until the sauce thickens. Stir occasionally with a wooden spoon to prevent the sauce from sticking to the base of the wok or frying pan.

5 Shallow fry the prawns until they turn pink. Alternatively, thread the prawns on to skewers and cook under a hot grill (broiler) for 2 minutes on each side.

6 Remove the cinnamon stick from the sauce and discard. Arrange the prawns on a warmed platter, garnish with spring onions and coriander leaves and sliced red chillies, if liked, and serve with skewers for using to dunk into the sauce.

VARIATIONS
• For a curry-style dish, heat the oil in a wok or large frying pan. Add the prawns (shrimp) and stir-fry for 3–4 minutes, or until pink. Mix the prawns with the sauce and serve with jasmine rice.
• You can use this basic sauce for satay pork or chicken, too. With a sharp knife, cut pork fillet (tenderloin) or skinless, boneless chicken breast portions into long thin strips and stir-fry in hot oil until golden brown all over and cooked through. Then stir into the sauce, instead of the king prawns (jumbo shrimp).
• You could use Thai red or green curry paste for this recipe. Make your own or buy a good-quality product from an Asian food store. Once opened, jars of curry paste should be kept in the refrigerator and used within 2 months.
• You can make the satay sauce in advance and leave it to cool. Transfer to a bowl, cover with clear film (plastic wrap) and store in the refrigerator. Reheat gently, stirring occasionally, before stir-frying the prawns (shrimp).

Energy 1042Kcal/4361kJ; Protein 59.7g; Carbohydrate 61.7g, of which sugars 53.1g; Fat 63.7g, of which saturates 13.1g; Cholesterol 472mg; Calcium 408mg; Fibre 7.5g; Sodium 3255mg.

SPICED SCALLOPS AND SUGAR SNAP PEAS ON CRISPY NOODLE CAKES

TENDER, JUICY SCALLOPS AND SUGAR SNAP PEAS COOKED IN SPICES AND SERVED ON A BED OF FRIED NOODLES IS A WINNING COMBINATION. IT'S SIMPLE AND STYLISH AND MAKES A GREAT DISH FOR SPECIAL-OCCASION ENTERTAINING.

SERVES FOUR

INGREDIENTS
  45ml/3 tbsp oyster sauce
  10ml/2 tsp soy sauce
  5ml/1 tsp sesame oil
  5ml/1 tsp golden caster
    (superfine) sugar
  30ml/2 tbsp sunflower oil
  2 fresh red chillies, finely sliced
  4 garlic cloves, finely chopped
  10ml/2 tsp finely chopped fresh
    root ginger
  250g/9oz sugar snap peas, trimmed
  500g/1¼lb king scallops, cleaned,
    roes discarded and sliced in half
  3 spring onions (scallions),
    finely shredded
For the noodle cakes
  250g/9oz fresh thin egg noodles
  10ml/2 tsp sesame oil
  120ml/4fl oz/½ cup sunflower oil

1 Cook the noodles in a wok of boiling water for 1 minute, or until tender. Drain well and transfer to a bowl with the sesame oil and 15ml/1 tbsp of the sunflower oil. Spread the noodles out on a large baking sheet and leave to dry in a warm place for 1 hour.

VARIATION
Use king prawns (jumbo shrimp) instead of scallops, if you like.

2 To cook the noodles, heat 15ml/ 1 tbsp of the oil in a non-stick wok over a high heat. Divide the noodle mixture into four portions and add one portion to the wok. Using a spatula, flatten it out and shape it into a cake.

3 Reduce the heat slightly and cook the cake for about 5 minutes on each side, or until crisp and golden. Drain on kitchen paper and keep warm while you make the remaining three noodle cakes in the same way.

4 Mix together the oyster sauce, soy sauce, sesame oil and sugar in a small bowl, stirring until the sugar has dissolved completely.

5 Heat a wok over medium heat and add the sunflower oil. When hot add the chillies, garlic and ginger, and stir-fry for 30 seconds. Add the sugar snap peas and stir-fry for 1–2 minutes.

6 Add the scallops and spring onions to the wok and stir fry over high heat for 1 minute. Stir in the oyster sauce mixture and cook for a further 1 minute until warmed through.

7 To serve, place a noodle cake on each of four warmed plates and top each one with the scallop mixture. Serve immediately.

Energy 689Kcal/2888kJ; Protein 41.4g; Carbohydrate 59.9g, of which sugars 6.2g; Fat 33.3g, of which saturates 5.4g; Cholesterol 78mg; Calcium 73mg; Fibre 5g; Sodium 700mg.

STEAMED SCALLOPS WITH GINGER

IT HELPS TO HAVE TWO WOKS WHEN MAKING THIS DISH. IF YOU ARE NOT DOUBLY BLESSED, BORROW AN EXTRA ONE FROM A FRIEND, OR USE A LARGE, HEAVY PAN WITH A TRIVET FOR STEAMING THE SECOND PLATE OF SCALLOPS. TAKE CARE NOT TO OVERCOOK THE TENDER SEAFOOD.

SERVES FOUR

INGREDIENTS
   24 king scallops in their
     shells, cleaned
   15ml/1 tbsp very finely shredded
     fresh root ginger
   5ml/1 tsp very finely chopped garlic
   1 large fresh red chilli, seeded and
     very finely chopped
   15ml/1 tbsp light soy sauce
   15ml/1 tbsp Chinese
     rice wine
   a few drops of sesame oil
   2–3 spring onions (scallions), very
     finely shredded
   15ml/1 tbsp very finely chopped
     fresh chives
   noodles or rice, to serve

1 Remove the scallops from their shells, then remove the membrane and hard white muscle from each one. Arrange the scallops on two plates. Rinse the shells, dry and set aside.

2 Fill two woks with 5cm/2in water and place a trivet in the base of each one. Bring to the boil.

3 Meanwhile, mix together the ginger, garlic, chilli, soy sauce, rice wine, sesame oil, spring onions and chives.

COOK'S TIP
Use the freshest scallops you can find. If you ask your fishmonger to shuck them, remember to ask for the shells.

4 Spoon the flavourings over the scallops. Lower a plate into each of the woks. Turn the heat to low, cover and steam for 10–12 minutes.

5 Divide the scallops among four, or eight, of the reserved shells and serve immediately with noodles or rice.

Energy 167Kcal/708kJ; Protein 29.8g; Carbohydrate 7g, of which sugars 2.6g; Fat 2g, of which saturates 0.6g; Cholesterol 59mg; Calcium 53mg; Fibre 0.8g; Sodium 496mg.

LANGOUSTINES WITH LEMON GRASS RISOTTO

THE WOK IS WONDERFUL FOR MAKING RISOTTO. FOR THIS VERSION, THE TRADITIONAL ITALIAN RISOTTO IS GIVEN A SUBTLE ASIAN TWIST WITH THE ADDITION OF FRAGRANT LEMON GRASS, ASIAN FISH SAUCE AND CHINESE CHIVES: THE PERFECT ACCOMPANIMENT TO SIMPLY STEAMED LANGOUSTINES.

SERVES FOUR

INGREDIENTS
    8 fresh langoustines
    30ml/2 tbsp olive oil
    15ml/1 tbsp butter
    1 onion, finely chopped
    1 carrot, finely diced
    1 celery stick, finely diced
    30ml/2 tbsp very finely chopped
        lemon grass
    300g/11oz/1½ cups arborio or other
        risotto rice
    200ml/7fl oz/scant 1 cup
        dry white wine
    1.5 litres/2½ pints/6¼ cups boiling
        vegetable stock
    50ml/2fl oz/¼ cup Thai fish sauce
    30ml/2 tbsp finely chopped
        Chinese chives
    salt and ground black pepper

1 Place the langoustines in a baking parchment-lined bamboo steamer, cover and place over a wok of simmering water. Steam for 6–8 minutes, remove from the heat and keep warm.

2 Heat the oil and butter in a wok and add the vegetables. Cook over a high heat for 2–3 minutes. Add the lemon grass and rice and stir-fry for 2 minutes.

3 Add the wine to the wok, reduce the heat and slowly stir until the wine is absorbed. Add about two thirds of the stock and cook gently, stirring until absorbed. Continue adding the stock, stirring until absorbed before adding more. When the rice is tender, stir in the fish sauce and Chinese chives, check the seasoning and serve immediately, topped with langoustines.

Energy 467Kcal/1949kJ; Protein 23.8g; Carbohydrate 64.2g, of which sugars 3.4g; Fat 8.9g, of which saturates 2.3g; Cholesterol 201mg; Calcium 114mg; Fibre 0.9g; Sodium 218mg.

STIR-FRIED SQUID <u>WITH</u> GINGER

THERE'S AN ANCIENT BELIEF THAT A WELL-LOVED WOK HOLDS THE MEMORY OF ALL THE DISHES THAT HAVE EVER BEEN COOKED IN IT. GIVE YOURS SOMETHING TO THINK ABOUT BY INTRODUCING IT TO THIS CLASSIC COMBINATION OF BABY SQUID IN SOY SAUCE, GINGER AND LEMON JUICE.

SERVES TWO

INGREDIENTS

    4 ready-prepared baby squid, total
       weight about 250g/9oz
    15ml/1 tbsp vegetable oil
    2 garlic cloves, finely chopped
    30ml/2 tbsp soy sauce
    2.5cm/1in piece fresh root ginger,
       peeled and finely chopped
    juice of ½ lemon
    5ml/1 tsp granulated sugar
    2 spring onions (scallions), chopped

VARIATIONS

This dish is often prepared with fresh galangal rather than ginger and works well with most kinds of seafood, including prawns (shrimp) and scallops.

1 Rinse the squid well and pat dry with kitchen paper. Cut the bodies into rings and halve the tentacles, if necessary.

2 Heat the oil in a wok or frying pan and cook the garlic until golden brown, but do not let it burn. Add the squid and stir-fry for 30 seconds over a high heat.

3 Add the soy sauce, ginger, lemon juice, sugar and spring onions. Stir-fry for a further 30 seconds, then serve.

COOK'S TIP

Squid has an undeserved reputation for being rubbery in texture. This is always a result of overcooking it.

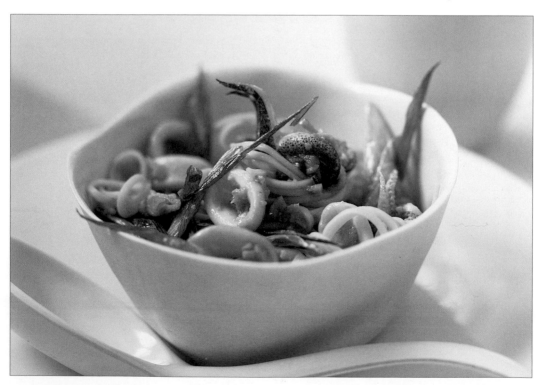

Energy 165Kcal/694kJ; Protein 19.7g; Carbohydrate 4.8g, of which sugars 3.2g; Fat 7.6g, of which saturates 1.2g; Cholesterol 281mg; Calcium 20mg; Fibre 0g; Sodium 1206mg.

STEAMED MUSSELS ^{IN} COCONUT MILK

MUSSELS STEAMED IN COCONUT MILK AND FRESH AROMATIC HERBS AND SPICES MAKE AN IDEAL DISH FOR INFORMAL ENTERTAINING. IT IS QUICK AND EASY TO MAKE IN A WOK, AND IS GREAT FOR A RELAXED DINNER WITH FRIENDS. SERVE WITH PLENTY OF CRUSTY BREAD.

SERVES FOUR

INGREDIENTS
15ml/1 tbsp sunflower oil
6 garlic cloves, roughly chopped
15ml/1 tbsp finely chopped
  fresh root ginger
2 large fresh red chillies, seeded
  and finely sliced
6 spring onions (scallions),
  finely chopped
400ml/14fl oz/1⅔ cups coconut milk
45ml/3 tbsp light soy sauce
2 limes
5ml/1 tsp caster (superfine) sugar
1.6kg/3½lb mussels, scrubbed
  and beards removed
a large handful of chopped
  coriander (cilantro)
salt and ground black pepper

1 Heat the wok over a high heat and then add the oil. Stir in the garlic, ginger, chillies and spring onions and stir-fry for 30 seconds. Pour in the coconut milk, then add the soy sauce.

2 Grate the zest of the limes into the coconut milk mixture and add the sugar. Stir to mix and bring to the boil.

3 Add the cleaned mussels. Return to the boil, cover and cook briskly for 5–6 minutes, or until all the mussels have opened. Discard any mussels that remain closed.

4 Remove the wok from the heat and stir the chopped coriander into the mussel mixture.

5 Season the mussels well with salt and pepper. Ladle into warmed bowls and serve immediately.

COOK'S TIP
For an informal supper with friends, take the wok straight to the table rather than serving in individual bowls. A wok makes a great serving dish, and there's something utterly irresistible about eating the mussels straight from it.

Energy 165Kcal/702kJ; Protein 21.9g; Carbohydrate 7.7g, of which sugars 7.6g; Fat 5.6g, of which saturates 1g; Cholesterol 48mg; Calcium 276mg; Fibre 0.3g; Sodium 1165mg.

SOTONG SAMBAL

SQUID IS READILY AVAILABLE THESE DAYS, AND IT NOW COMES CLEANED, WHICH IS A DEFINITE BONUS. WASH THOROUGHLY INSIDE THE POCKET TO MAKE SURE THAT ALL THE QUILL HAS BEEN REMOVED.

SERVES TWO

INGREDIENTS
    8 small squid, each about 10cm/4in
       long, total weight about 350g/12oz
    lime juice (optional)
    salt
    boiled rice, to serve
For the stuffing
    175g/6oz white fish fillets, such as
       sole or plaice, skinned
    2.5cm/1in piece fresh root ginger,
       peeled and finely sliced
    2 spring onions (scallions), finely
       chopped
    50g/2oz peeled cooked prawns
       (shrimp), roughly chopped
For the sambal sauce
    4 macadamia nuts or
       blanched almonds
    1cm/$\frac{1}{2}$in piece fresh galangal,
       peeled, or 5ml/1 tsp drained
       bottled galangal
    2 lemon grass stalks, root trimmed
    1cm/$\frac{1}{2}$in cube shrimp paste
    4 fresh red chillies, or to taste,
       seeded and roughly chopped
    175g/6oz small onions, roughly
       chopped
    60–90ml/4–6 tbsp vegetable oil
    400ml/14fl oz can coconut milk

2 To make the stuffing, put the fish, ginger and spring onions in a mortar. Add a little salt and pound to a paste. Use a food processor to grind the mixture, if you like, but don't retain a little texture and don't overprocess.

3 Transfer the fish mixture to a bowl and stir in the prawns.

4 Divide the filling among the squid, using a spoon or a forcing bag fitted with a plain tube to fill them. Tuck the tentacles into the stuffing and secure the top of each squid with a cocktail stick, to stop the filling escaping.

5 Make the sauce. Put the macadamia nuts or almonds and galangal in a food processor. Cut off the lower 5cm/2in from the lemon grass stalks, chop them roughly and add them to the processor with the shrimp paste, chillies and onions. Process to a paste.

6 Heat the oil in a wok and fry the mixture to bring out the full flavours. Bruise the remaining lemon grass and add it to the wok with the coconut milk. Stir constantly until the sauce comes to the boil, then lower the heat and simmer the sauce for 5 minutes.

7 Arrange the squid in the sauce, and cook for 15–20 minutes. Taste and season with salt and lime juice, if liked. Serve with boiled rice.

Energy 538Kcal/2253kJ; Protein 50.4g; Carbohydrate 19.6g, of which sugars 15.4g; Fat 29.4g, of which saturates 4g; Cholesterol 483mg; Calcium 148mg; Fibre 1.8g; Sodium 517mg.

DEEP-FRIED PLAICE

IN THIS DISH, CALLED KAREI KARA-AGÉ, *THE FLESH OF THE FISH AND ALSO THE SKELETON IS DEEP-FRIED TO SUCH CRISPNESS THAT YOU CAN EAT THE BONES, TAILS AND HEADS, IF YOU LIKE.*

SERVES FOUR

INGREDIENTS
    4 small plaice or flounder, about
        500–675g/1¼–1½lb total weight,
        gutted, not trimmed
    60ml/4 tbsp cornflour (cornstarch)
    vegetable oil, for deep-frying
    salt
For the condiment
    130g/4½oz mooli (daikon), peeled
    4 dried chillies, seeded
    1 bunch of chives, finely chopped
        (to make 50ml/2fl oz/¼ cup)
For the sauce
    20ml/4 tsp rice vinegar
    20ml/4 tsp shoyu

1 Wash the fish under running water and put on a chopping board. Use a very sharp knife to make deep cuts around the gills and across the tail. Cut through the skin from the head down to the tail along the centre of the fish. Slide the knife under the cut near the head and gently cut the fillet from the bone. Fold the fillet with your hand as you cut as if peeling the fillet from the bone. Keep the knife horizontal to the fish.

2 Repeat for the other half, then turn the fish over and do the same to get four fillets from each fish. Place in a dish and sprinkle with a little salt on both sides. Keep the bony skeletons.

3 Pierce the mooli with a skewer or a chopstick in four places to make holes, then insert the chillies. After 15 minutes grate finely.

4 Squeeze out the moisture by hand. Scoop a quarter of the grated mooli and chilli into an egg cup, then press with your fingers. Turn out the cup on to a plate. Make three more mounds.

5 Mix the rice vinegar and shoyu and put in a bowl.

6 Cut the fish fillets into four slices crossways and put into a plastic bag with the cornflour. Shake gently to coat. Heat the oil in a wok or pan to 180°C/350°F, or until a cube of bread, dropped into the oil, browns in 40 seconds. Fry the fillets, two to three at a time, until light golden brown.

7 Raise the temperature of the oil to 190°C/375°F. Dust the skeletons with cornflour and slide into the oil.

8 Cook until golden, drain on a wire rack for 5 minutes, then fry again until very crisp. Drain and sprinkle with salt.

9 Arrange the skeletons and fried fish on the plates. Put the mooli and chives to one side on each plate. Have small plates for the sauce. To eat, mix the condiment with the sauce and dip the fillets and bones into the sauce.

Energy 331Kcal/1378kJ; Protein 19.7g; Carbohydrate 16.2g, of which sugars 1.2g; Fat 21.2g, of which saturates 2.6g; Cholesterol 0mg; Calcium 120mg; Fibre 1.2g; Sodium 640mg.

Sweet and Sour Fish

When fish such as red mullet or snapper is deep-fried in oil the skin becomes crisp, while the flesh inside remains moist and juicy. The sweet and sour sauce in this dish, with its colourful cherry tomatoes, perfectly complements the fish.

SERVES FOUR TO SIX

INGREDIENTS

    1 large or 2 medium fish, such as
      snapper or mullet, cleaned with
      heads removed
    20ml/4 tsp cornflour (cornstarch)
    120ml/4fl oz/½ cup vegetable oil
    15ml/1 tbsp chopped garlic
    15ml/1 tbsp chopped fresh ginger
    30ml/2 tbsp chopped shallots
    225g/8oz cherry tomatoes
    30ml/2 tbsp red wine vinegar
    30ml/2 tbsp granulated sugar
    30ml/2 tbsp tomato ketchup
    15ml/1 tbsp Thai fish sauce
    45ml/3 tbsp water
    salt and ground black pepper
    coriander (cilantro) leaves and
      shredded spring onions
      (scallions), to garnish

1 Rinse and dry the fish. Score the skin diagonally on both sides, then coat the fish lightly all over with 15ml/1 tbsp of the cornflour. Shake off any excess.

2 Heat the oil in a wok or large frying pan. Add the fish and cook over a medium heat for 6–7 minutes. Turn the fish over and cook for 6–7 minutes more, until it is crisp and brown.

3 Remove the fish with a metal spatula or fish slice and place on a large platter. Pour off all but 30ml/2 tbsp of the oil from the wok or pan and reheat. Add the garlic, ginger and shallots and cook over a medium heat, stirring occasionally, for 3–4 minutes, until golden.

4 Add the cherry tomatoes and cook until they burst open. Stir in the vinegar, sugar, tomato ketchup and fish sauce. Lower the heat and simmer gently for 1–2 minutes, then taste and adjust the seasoning, adding more vinegar, sugar and/or fish sauce, if necessary.

5 In a cup, mix the remaining 5ml/1 tsp cornflour to a paste with the water. Stir into the sauce. Heat, stirring, until it thickens. Pour the sauce over the fish, garnish with coriander leaves and shredded spring onions and serve.

Energy 245Kcal/1023kJ; Protein 16.2g; Carbohydrate 14.8g, of which sugars 10.6g; Fat 13.8g, of which saturates 1.6g; Cholesterol 38mg; Calcium 27mg; Fibre 1.1g; Sodium 138mg.

STEAMED FISH <u>WITH</u> CHILLI SAUCE

A LARGE WOK IS IDEAL FOR STEAMING FISH. BY LEAVING THE FISH WHOLE AND ON THE BONE, MAXIMUM FLAVOUR IS RETAINED AND THE FLESH REMAINS BEAUTIFULLY MOIST. THE BANANA LEAF IS BOTH AUTHENTIC AND ATTRACTIVE, BUT YOU CAN USE BAKING PARCHMENT INSTEAD.

SERVES FOUR

INGREDIENTS

    1 large or 2 medium firm fish such
      as sea bass or grouper, scaled
      and cleaned
    30ml/2 tbsp rice wine
    3 fresh red chillies, seeded and
      thinly sliced
    2 garlic cloves, finely chopped
    2cm/¾ in piece fresh root ginger,
      peeled and finely shredded
    2 lemon grass stalks, crushed and
      finely chopped
    2 spring onions
      (scallions), chopped
    30ml/2 tbsp Thai fish sauce
    juice of 1 lime
    1 fresh banana leaf
For the chilli sauce
    10 fresh red chillies, seeded
      and chopped
    4 garlic cloves, chopped
    60ml/4 tbsp Thai fish sauce
    15ml/1 tbsp granulated sugar
    75ml/5 tbsp fresh lime juice

1 Thoroughly rinse the fish under cold running water. Pat it dry with kitchen paper. With a sharp knife, slash the skin of the fish a few times on both sides.

2 Mix together the rice wine, chillies, garlic, shredded ginger, lemon grass and spring onions in a non-metallic bowl. Add the fish sauce and lime juice and mix to a paste. Place the fish on the banana leaf and spread the spice paste evenly over it, rubbing it in well where the skin has been slashed.

3 Put a rack or a small upturned plate in the base of a wok. Pour in boiling water to a depth of 5cm/2in. Lift the banana leaf, together with the fish, and place it on the rack or plate. Cover with a lid and steam for 10–15 minutes, or until the fish is cooked.

4 Meanwhile, make the sauce. Place all the ingredients in a food processor and process until smooth. If the mixture seems to be too thick, add a little cold water. Scrape into a serving bowl.

5 Serve the fish hot, on the banana leaf if you like, with the sweet chilli sauce to spoon over the top.

Energy 228Kcal/960kJ; Protein 35.2g; Carbohydrate 12g, of which sugars 10.1g; Fat 4.7g, of which saturates 0.7g; Cholesterol 140mg; Calcium 254mg; Fibre 1.6g; Sodium 392mg.

FRAGRANT RED SNAPPER IN BANANA LEAVES

SHINY, DARK GREEN BANANA LEAVES MAKE A REALLY GOOD WRAPPING FOR FISH THAT IS STEAMED IN THE WOK. HERE, WHOLE SNAPPERS ARE INFUSED WITH A DELIGHTFUL MIX OF COCONUT CREAM, MINT, CORIANDER, KAFFIR LIME LEAVES, LEMON GRASS AND CHILLI TO MAKE AN IMPRESSIVE MAIN COURSE.

3 Place the coconut cream, chopped herbs, lime juice, spring onions, lime leaves and chillies in a bowl and stir well. Season with salt and pepper.

4 Lay each banana leaf out flat on a work surface and place a fish and a split lemon grass stalk in the centre of each of them. Spread the herb mixture over each fish.

5 Wrap the banana leaf around each one to form four neat parcels. Secure each parcel tightly with a bamboo skewer or a cocktail stick (toothpick).

6 Place the parcels in a single layer in one or two tiers of a large bamboo steamer and place over a wok of simmering water. Cover tightly and steam for 15–20 minutes, or until the fish is cooked through.

7 Remove the fish from the steamer and serve immediately, still in their banana-leaf wrappings, with steamed rice and steamed Asian greens.

COOK'S TIP
When you spread the spicy coconut cream mixture over the fish, work the mixture into the cuts that you have made. This allows the flavours to penetrate the flesh and gives the finished dish a fabulous flavour. If you have time, leave the fish to stand for about half an hour before steaming. Swap the steamer baskets over halfway through cooking, so each gets similar exposure to maximum heat.

SERVES FOUR

INGREDIENTS
- 4 small red snapper, grouper, tilapia or red bream, gutted and cleaned
- 4 large squares of banana leaf (approximately 30cm/12in square)
- 50ml/2fl oz/¼ cup coconut cream
- 90ml/6 tbsp chopped coriander (cilantro)
- 90ml/6 tbsp chopped mint
- juice of 3 limes
- 3 spring onions (scallions), finely sliced
- 4 kaffir lime leaves, finely shredded
- 2 red chillies, seeded and finely sliced
- 4 lemon grass stalks, split lengthways
- salt and ground black pepper
- steamed rice and steamed Asian greens, to serve

1 Using a small sharp knife, score the fish diagonally on each side. Half fill a wok with water and bring to the boil.

2 Dip each square of banana leaf into the boiling water in the wok for 15–20 seconds so they become pliable. Lift out carefully, rinse under cold water and dry with kitchen paper.

Energy 185Kcal/781kJ; Protein 39.4g; Carbohydrate 0.9g, of which sugars 0.8g; Fat 2.7g, of which saturates 0.6g; Cholesterol 74mg; Calcium 87mg; Fibre 0.1g; Sodium 168mg.

STEAMED FISH SKEWERS ᴼᴺ RICE NOODLES

FRESH TROUT IS PERFECT FOR SUMMER ENTERTAINING. IN THIS RECIPE, SUCCULENT FILLETS ARE MARINATED IN A TANGY CITRUS SPICE BLEND, THEN SKEWERED AND STEAMED IN THE WOK BEFORE SERVING ON A BED OF FRAGRANT HERB NOODLES, FLAVOURED WITH CHILLI AND SPRING ONIONS.

SERVES FOUR

INGREDIENTS
    4 trout fillets, skinned
    2.5ml/½ tsp turmeric
    15ml/1 tbsp mild curry paste
    juice of 2 lemons
    15ml/1 tbsp sunflower oil
    salt and ground black pepper
    45ml/3 tbsp chilli-roasted peanuts,
        roughly chopped
    chopped fresh mint, to garnish
For the noodles
    300g/11oz rice noodles
    15ml/1 tbsp sunflower oil
    1 red chilli, seeded
        and finely sliced
    4 spring onions (scallions),
        cut into slivers
    60ml/4 tbsp roughly chopped
        fresh mint
    60ml/4 tbsp roughly chopped
        fresh sweet basil

1 Trim each fillet and place in a large bowl. Mix together the turmeric, curry paste, lemon juice and oil and pour over the fish. Season with salt and black pepper and toss to mix well.

2 Place the rice noodles in a bowl and pour over enough boiling water to cover. Leave to soak for 3–4 minutes and then drain. Refresh in cold water, drain and set aside.

3 Thread 2 bamboo skewers through each trout fillet and arrange in two tiers of a bamboo steamer lined with baking parchment.

4 Cover the steamer and place over a wok of simmering water (making sure the water doesn't touch the steamer). Steam the fish skewers for 5–6 minutes, or until the fish is just cooked through.

5 Meanwhile, in a clean wok heat the oil. Add the chilli, spring onions and drained noodles and stir-fry for about 2 minutes and then stir in the chopped herbs. Season with salt and ground black pepper and divide among four bowls or plates.

6 Top each bowl of noodles with a steamed fish skewer and scatter over the chilli-roasted peanuts. Garnish with chopped mint and serve immediately.

VARIATION
You can grill (broil) these fillets instead of steaming, if you prefer. If you do use the grill (broiler), you need to soak the bamboo skewers in cold water for at least 30 minutes before threading them through the trout fillets. This will prevent them burning during cooking.

Energy 555Kcal/2317kJ; Protein 36g; Carbohydrate 62.8g, of which sugars 1g; Fat 16.6g, of which saturates 1.6g; Cholesterol 0mg; Calcium 52mg; Fibre 1.3g; Sodium 97mg.

MACKEREL <u>WITH</u> MUSHROOMS <u>AND</u> BLACK BEANS

EARTHY-TASTING SHIITAKE MUSHROOMS, ZESTY FRESH GINGER AND PUNGENT SALTED BLACK BEANS ARE THE PERFECT PARTNERS FOR ROBUSTLY FLAVOURED MACKEREL FILLETS. THE STRIKING COMBINATION OF FLAVOURS ALL COME TOGETHER BEAUTIFULLY.

SERVES FOUR

INGREDIENTS
    8 x 115g/4oz mackerel fillets
    20 dried shiitake mushrooms
    15ml/1 tbsp finely julienned fresh
       root ginger
    3 star anise
    45ml/3 tbsp dark soy sauce
    15ml/1 tbsp Chinese rice wine
    15ml/1 tbsp salted black beans
    6 spring onions (scallions), finely
       shredded
    30ml/2 tbsp sunflower oil
    5ml/1 tsp sesame oil
    4 garlic cloves, very thinly sliced
       sliced cucumber and steamed
       basmati rice, to serve

1 Divide the mackerel fillets between two lightly oiled heatproof plates, with the skin-side up. Using a small, sharp knife, make 3–4 diagonal slits in each one, then set aside.

2 Place the dried shiitake mushrooms in a large bowl and pour over enough boiling water to cover. Leave to soak for 20–25 minutes. Drain, reserving the soaking liquid, discard the stems and slice the caps thinly.

3 Place a trivet or a steamer rack in a large wok and pour in 5cm/2in of the mushroom liquid (top up with water if necessary). Add half the ginger and the star anise.

COOK'S TIP
If the mackerel has been cleaned but you need to fillet it, this is very easy to do. Just open the fish up like a book, lay it on a board with the skin side uppermost, and press down firmly with your fingers all along the backbone. Turn the fish over and the backbone will come away easily. Remove any stray bones with tweezers and cut off the tail.

4 Push the remaining ginger strips into the slits in the fish and scatter over the sliced mushrooms. Bring the liquid in the wok to a boil and lower one of the prepared plates on to the trivet.

5 Cover the wok, reduce the heat and steam for 10–12 minutes, or until the mackerel is cooked. Remove the plate and repeat with the second plate of fish, adding liquid to the wok if necessary.

6 Transfer the steamed fish to a serving platter and keep warm. Ladle 105ml/7 tbsp of the steaming liquid into a clean wok with the soy sauce, wine and black beans, place over a gentle heat and bring to a simmer. Spoon over the fish and sprinkle over the spring onions.

7 Wipe out the wok with a piece of kitchen paper and place over a medium heat. Add the oils and garlic and stir-fry for a few minutes until lightly golden. Pour over the fish and serve with sliced cucumber and steamed basmati rice.

Energy 573Kcal/2378kJ; Protein 43.9g; Carbohydrate 3.2g, of which sugars 1.1g; Fat 42.7g, of which saturates 8.2g; Cholesterol 122mg; Calcium 37mg; Fibre 1.2g; Sodium 678mg.

DEEP-FRIED SKATE WINGS WITH WASABI

WHOLE SKATE WINGS DIPPED IN A TEMPURA BATTER AND DEEP-FRIED UNTIL CRISP AND GOLDEN LOOK STUNNING AND TASTE WONDERFUL. THE CREAMY, ZESTY MAYONNAISE FLAVOURED WITH SOY SAUCE, FIERY WASABI PASTE AND SPRING ONIONS MAKES A GREAT ACCOMPANIMENT.

SERVES FOUR

INGREDIENTS

  4 x 250g/9oz skate wings
  65g/2½oz/9 tbsp cornflour
    (cornstarch)
  65g/2½oz/9 tbsp plain
    (all-purpose) flour
  5ml/1 tsp salt
  5ml/1 tsp Chinese five-spice powder
  15ml/1 tbsp sesame seeds
  200ml/7fl oz/scant 1 cup ice-cold
    soda water
  sunflower oil, for frying
For the mayonnaise
  200ml/7fl oz/scant 1 cup mayonnaise
  15ml/1 tbsp light soy sauce
  finely grated rind and juice of 1 lime
  5ml/1 tsp wasabi
  15ml/1 tbsp finely chopped spring
    onion (scallion)

1 Using kitchen scissors, trim away the frill from the edges of the skate wings and discard. Set aside.

2 In a large mixing bowl combine the cornflour, plain flour, salt, five-spice powder and sesame seeds. Gradually pour in the soda water and stir to mix. (It will be quite lumpy.)

3 Fill a large wok one-third full of sunflower oil and heat to 190°C/375°F or until a cube of bread, dropped into the oil, browns in 40 seconds.

4 One at a time, dip the skate wings in the batter, then lower them carefully into the wok and deep-fry for 4–5 minutes, until the skate is fully cooked and crispy. Drain on kitchen paper. Set aside and keep warm.

5 Meanwhile, mix together all the mayonnaise ingredients and divide among four small bowls. Serve immediately with the skate wings.

COOK'S TIP
Look for packets of tempura batter mix at health food stores and Asian markets. It doesn't take long to make your own batter, but sometimes seconds count.

Energy 705Kcal/2921kJ; Protein 31.9g; Carbohydrate 11.7g, of which sugars 1.2g; Fat 59.3g, of which saturates 11g; Cholesterol 38mg; Calcium 112mg; Fibre 0.5g; Sodium 792mg.

FISH MOOLIE

THIS IS A VERY POPULAR SOUTH-EAST ASIAN FISH CURRY IN A COCONUT SAUCE, WHICH IS TRULY DELICIOUS. CHOOSE A FIRM-TEXTURED FISH SO THAT THE PIECES STAY INTACT DURING THE BRIEF COOKING PROCESS. HALIBUT AND COD WORK EQUALLY WELL.

SERVES FOUR

INGREDIENTS

- 500g/1¼lb monkfish or other firm-textured fish fillets, skinned and cut into 2.5cm/1in cubes
- 2.5ml/½ tsp salt
- 50g/2oz/⅔ cup desiccated (dry unsweetened shredded) coconut
- 6 shallots or small onions, chopped
- 6 blanched almonds
- 2–3 garlic cloves, roughly chopped
- 2.5cm/1in piece fresh root ginger, peeled and sliced
- 2 lemon grass stalks, trimmed
- 10ml/2 tsp ground turmeric
- 45ml/3 tbsp vegetable oil
- 2 × 400ml/14fl oz cans coconut milk
- 1–3 fresh chillies, seeded and sliced
- salt and ground black pepper
- fresh chives, to garnish
- boiled rice, to serve

1 Spread out the pieces of fish in a shallow dish and sprinkle them with the salt. Dry-fry the coconut in a wok or large frying pan over medium heat, stirring constantly until it is crisp. Put in a food processor, process to an oily paste and transfer to a bowl.

2 Add the shallots or onions, almonds, garlic and ginger to the food processor. Chop the lower 5cm/2in of the lemon grass stalks and add to the processor. Process the mixture to a paste. Add the turmeric and process briefly to mix. Bruise the remaining lemon grass and set the stalks aside.

3 Heat the oil in a wok. Add the onion mixture and cook for a few minutes without browning. Stir in the coconut milk and bring to the boil, stirring constantly to prevent curdling.

4 Add the fish, most of the sliced chilli and the bruised lemon grass stalks. Cook for 3–4 minutes. Stir in the coconut paste and cook for a further 2–3 minutes only. Do not overcook the fish. Taste and adjust the seasoning.

5 Remove the lemon grass. Transfer to a hot serving dish and sprinkle with the remaining chilli. Garnish with chives and serve with boiled rice.

Energy 319Kcal/1335kJ; Protein 22.4g; Carbohydrate 16.7g, of which sugars 14.9g; Fat 18.6g, of which saturates 8.3g; Cholesterol 18mg; Calcium 96mg; Fibre 3g; Sodium 249mg.

SWEET DISHES AND DESSERTS

It may surprise you to discover just how many sweet dishes

can be cooked in the wok, from steamed custards to sweet rice

vermicelli. It is a practical pan for deep-fried treats such as

fritters and crispy wontons, since less oil is needed than for

conventional deep-frying, yet the wide bowl shape gives you a

good surface area. The wok can also be used for

poaching fruit, such as Vanilla, Honey and Saffron Pears, or

cooking desserts such as Caramelized Pineapple with Lemon

Grass. If you use a wok for cooking fruit, make sure it

has a non-stick surface, or the acidity may react with

the metal and cause discoloration.

STEAMED CUSTARD ᴵᴺ NECTARINES

STEAMING NECTARINES OR PEACHES IN THE WOK BRINGS OUT THEIR NATURAL COLOUR AND SWEETNESS, SO THIS IS A GOOD WAY OF MAKING THE MOST OF FRUIT THAT ISN'T QUITE AS RIPE AS IT COULD BE, OR WHICH NEEDS A FLAVOUR BOOST.

SERVES FOUR TO SIX

INGREDIENTS
  6 nectarines
  1 large (US extra large) egg
  45ml/3 tbsp palm sugar or light
    muscovado (brown) sugar
  30ml/2 tbsp coconut milk

COOK'S TIP
Palm sugar, also known as jaggery, is made from the sap of certain Asian palm trees, such as coconut and palmyrah. It is available from Asian food stores. If you buy it as a cake or large lump, you need to grate it before use. Light Muscovado sugar makes a good substitute as it has a similar, toffee-like flavour.

1 Cut the nectarines in half. Using a teaspoon, scoop out the stones (pits) and a little of the surrounding flesh.

2 Lightly beat the egg, then add the sugar and the coconut milk. Beat until the sugar has dissolved.

3 Transfer the nectarines to steamer tiers and carefully fill the cavities three-quarters full with the custard mixture. Steam over a pan of simmering water for 5–10 minutes. Remove from the heat and leave to cool completely before transferring to plates and serving.

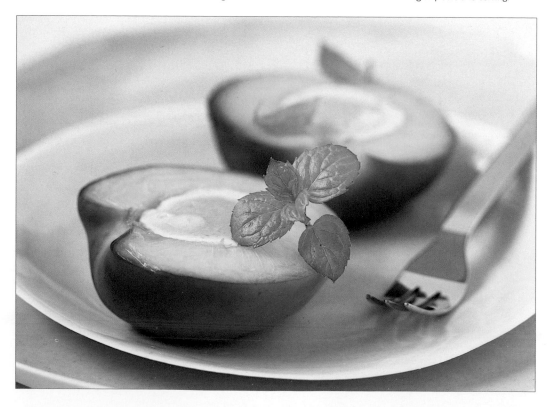

Energy 213Kcal/897kJ; Protein 12.6g; Carbohydrate 21.6g, of which sugars 21.6g; Fat 9.4g, of which saturates 2.6g; Cholesterol 317mg; Calcium 64mg; Fibre 1.8g; Sodium 124mg.

MANGO WONTONS ^{WITH} RASPBERRY SAUCE

*THESE CRISP, GOLDEN PARCELS FILLED WITH MELTINGLY SWEET, HOT MANGO ARE PERFECT FOR A
CASUAL SUPPER OR A SOPHISTICATED DINNER. THE SWEET RASPBERRY SAUCE LOOKS STUNNING
DRIZZLED OVER THE WONTONS AND TASTES EVEN BETTER. SERVE ANY EXTRA SAUCE IN A BOWL.*

SERVES FOUR

INGREDIENTS
    2 firm, ripe mangoes
    24 fresh wonton wrappers
        (approximately 7.5cm/3in square)
    oil, for deep-frying
    icing (confectioners') sugar, to dust
For the sauce
    400g/14oz/3½ cups raspberries
    45ml/3 tbsp icing
        (confectioners') sugar
    a squeeze of lemon juice

1 First make the sauce. Place the
raspberries and icing sugar in a food
processor and blend until smooth.

2 Press the raspberry purée through a
sieve (strainer) to remove the seeds,
then stir a squeeze of lemon juice into
the sauce. Cover and place in the
refrigerator until ready to serve.

3 Peel the mangoes, then carefully slice
the flesh away from one side of the flat
stone (pit). Repeat on the second side,
then trim off any remaining flesh from
around the stone. Cut the mango flesh
into 1cm/½in dice.

COOK'S TIP
To check that a mango is ripe, cup it
gently in your hand and give it a sniff. A
ripe mango will yield to the touch and
smell fragrant. Slightly unripe mangoes
will ripen if placed in a paper bag with a
banana for a day or two.

4 Lay 12 wonton wrappers on a clean
work surface and place 10ml/2 tsp of
the chopped mango in the centre
of each one. Brush the edges with water
and top with the remaining wonton
wrappers. Press the edges to seal.

5 Heat the oil in a wok to 180°C/350°F
or until a cube of bread, dropped into
the oil, browns in 45 seconds. Deep-fry
the wontons, 2–3 at a time, for about
2 minutes, or until crisp and golden.

6 Remove the cooked wontons from the
oil using a slotted spoon and drain on
kitchen paper. Dust with icing sugar
and serve on individual plates drizzled
with the raspberry sauce.

VARIATION
This also tastes good with apricot sauce.
Simply poach dried apricots in water or
apple juice until soft, then blitz the
apricots and cooking juice in a blender.

Energy 314Kcal/1331kJ; Protein 5.5g; Carbohydrate 56.1g, of which sugars 27.3g; Fat 9.2g, of which saturates 1.2g; Cholesterol 0mg; Calcium 93mg; Fibre 5.6g; Sodium 6mg.

CHINESE-STYLE TOFFEE APPLES

THIS CLASSIC DESSERT WILL MAKE A GREAT END TO ANY MEAL. WEDGES OF CRISP APPLE ARE ENCASED IN A LIGHT BATTER, THEN DIPPED IN CRISPY CARAMEL TO MAKE A SWEET, STICKY DESSERT THAT IS GUARANTEED TO GET STUCK IN YOUR TEETH! YOU CAN USE BABY BANANAS IN PLACE OF THE APPLES.

SERVES FOUR

INGREDIENTS
115g/4oz/1 cup plain
  (all-purpose) flour
10ml/2 tsp baking powder
60ml/4 tbsp cornflour (cornstarch)
4 firm apples
sunflower oil, for deep-frying
200g/7oz/1 cup caster
  (superfine) sugar

1 In a large mixing bowl, combine the flour, baking powder, cornflour and 175ml/6fl oz/¾ cup water. Stir to make a smooth batter and set aside.

2 Peel and core the apples, then cut each one into 8 thick wedges.

3 Fill a wok one-third full of sunflower oil and heat to 180°C/350°F or until a cube of bread, dropped into the oil, browns in 45 seconds.

4 Working quickly, in batches, dip the apple wedges in the batter, drain off any excess and deep-fry for 2 minutes, or until golden brown. Remove with a slotted spoon and place on kitchen paper to drain.

5 Reheat the oil to 180°C/350°F and fry the wedges for a second time, again giving them about 2 minutes. Drain well on kitchen paper and set aside.

6 Very carefully, pour off all but 30ml/ 2 tbsp of the oil from the wok and stir in the sugar. Heat gently until the sugar melts and starts to caramelize. When the mixture is light brown, add a few pieces of apple at a time and toss to coat evenly.

7 Fill a large bowl with ice cubes and chilled water. Plunge the coated apple pieces briefly into the iced water to harden the caramel, then remove with a slotted spoon and serve immediately.

COOK'S TIP
Don't cook the apples in advance or the caramel will soften.

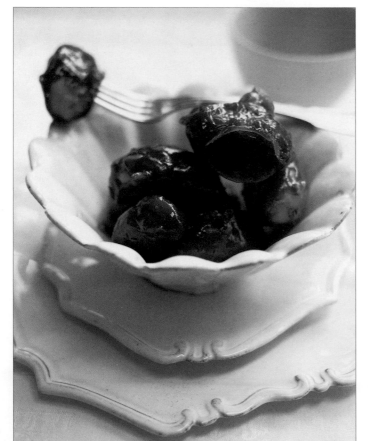

Energy 457Kcal/1940kJ; Protein 3.4g; Carbohydrate 97.3g, of which sugars 61.6g; Fat 8.8g, of which saturates 1.1g; Cholesterol 0mg; Calcium 73mg; Fibre 2.5g; Sodium 14mg.

SWEET AND SPICY RICE FRITTERS

THESE DELICIOUS LITTLE GOLDEN BALLS OF RICE ARE SCENTED WITH SWEET, WARM SPICES AND WILL FILL THE KITCHEN WITH WONDERFUL AROMAS WHILE YOU'RE COOKING. TO ENJOY THEM AT THEIR BEST, SERVE PIPING HOT, AS SOON AS YOU'VE DUSTED THEM WITH SUGAR.

SERVES FOUR

INGREDIENTS
175g/6oz cooked basmati rice
2 eggs, lightly beaten
60ml/4 tbsp caster (superfine) sugar
a pinch of nutmeg
2.5ml/½ tsp ground cinnamon
a pinch of ground cloves
10ml/2 tsp vanilla extract
50g/2oz/½ cup plain
  (all-purpose) flour
10ml/2 tsp baking powder
a pinch of salt
25g/1oz desiccated (dry unsweetened
  shredded) coconut
sunflower oil, for deep-frying
icing (confectioners') sugar,
  to dust

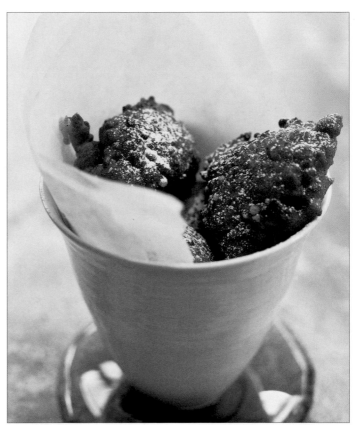

1 Place the cooked rice, eggs, sugar, nutmeg, cinnamon, cloves and vanilla extract in a large bowl and whisk together to combine.

2 Sift in the flour, baking powder and salt and add the coconut. Mix well until thoroughly combined.

3 Fill a wok one-third full of the oil and heat to 180°C/350°F or until a cube of bread, dropped into the oil, browns in 45 seconds.

4 Very gently, drop tablespoonfuls of the mixture into the oil, one at a time, and fry for 2–3 minutes, or until golden. Carefully remove the fritters from the wok using a slotted spoon and drain well on kitchen paper.

5 Divide the fritters into four portions, or simply pile them up on a single large platter. Dust them with icing sugar and serve immediately.

Energy 316Kcal/1321kJ; Protein 6.6g; Carbohydrate 45.8g, of which sugars 16.3g; Fat 12.4g, of which saturates 4.8g; Cholesterol 95mg; Calcium 46mg; Fibre 1.3g; Sodium 38mg.

Coconut and Mandarin Custards

THESE SCENTED CUSTARDS WITH A FABULOUS MELT-IN-THE-MOUTH TEXTURE ARE BEST SERVED WARM.
HOWEVER, THEY ARE ALSO DELICIOUS SERVED CHILLED, MAKING THEM PERFECT FOR HASSLE-FREE
ENTERTAINING. YOU CAN MAKE THE PRALINE A FEW DAYS IN ADVANCE.

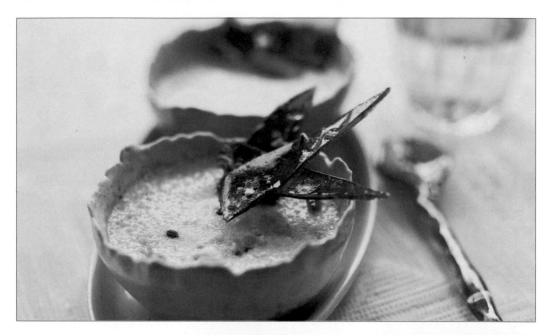

SERVES FOUR

INGREDIENTS
200ml/7fl oz/scant 1 cup
  coconut cream
200ml/7fl oz/scant 1 cup double
  (heavy) cream
2.5ml/½ tsp finely ground star anise
75ml/5 tbsp golden caster
  (superfine) sugar
15ml/1 tbsp very finely grated
  mandarin or orange rind
4 egg yolks
For the praline
175g/6oz/scant 1 cup caster
  (superfine) sugar
50g/2oz/½ cup roughly chopped
  mixed nuts (cashews, almonds and
  peanuts)

1 Make the praline. Place the sugar in a
non-stick wok with 15–30ml/1–2 tbsp
water. Cook over a medium heat until
the sugar dissolves and turns light gold.

2 Remove the syrup from the heat and
pour on to a baking sheet lined with
baking parchment. Spread out using the
back of a spoon, then sprinkle the
chopped nuts evenly over the top and
leave to harden.

3 Meanwhile place the coconut cream,
double cream, star anise, sugar,
mandarin or orange rind and egg yolks
in a large bowl. Whisk to combine and
pour the mixture into 4 lightly greased
ramekins or small, heatproof bowls.

4 Place the ramekins or cups in a large
steamer, cover and place in a wok and
steam over gently simmering water
for 12–15 minutes, or until the custards
are just set.

5 Carefully lift the custards from the
steamer and leave to cool slightly
for about 10 minutes.

6 To serve, break up the praline into
rough pieces and serve on top of, or
alongside, the custards.

Energy 643Kcal/2688kJ; Protein 6.7g; Carbohydrate 71g, of which sugars 69.3g; Fat 38.9g, of which saturates 19.6g; Cholesterol 270mg; Calcium 100mg; Fibre 0.4g; Sodium 115mg.

ORANGE AND DATE BUTTERMILK PANCAKES

SERVE THESE SWEET, STICKY, GOLDEN PANCAKES FOR BREAKFAST, BRUNCH OR DESSERT. THEY'RE BURSTING WITH THE FLAVOUR OF ZESTY ORANGE AND SWEET JUICY DATES AND ARE UTTERLY MOREISH. MEDJOOL DATES HAVE AN INTENSELY SWEET FLESH AND WILL GIVE THE BEST RESULTS.

SERVES FOUR

INGREDIENTS

150g/5oz/1¼ cups self-raising
   (self-rising) flour
2.5ml/½ tsp baking powder
a pinch of salt
250ml/8fl oz/1 cup buttermilk
3 eggs
15ml/1 tbsp caster
   (superfine) sugar
200g/7oz/1¼ cup Medjool
   dates, stoned (pitted)
finely grated rind and juice
   from 1 small orange
50g/2oz/¼ cup unsalted (sweet)
   butter, melted
sunflower oil, for greasing
clear honey, to drizzle
natural (plain) yogurt,
   to serve

1 Sift the flour and baking soda into a large bowl with a pinch of salt. Whisk in the buttermilk, eggs, sugar, dates, orange rind and juice and melted butter. Leave to stand for 15 minutes.

2 Brush a wok with a little oil and heat over a medium heat. When hot, pour a small ladleful of the mixture into the wok. Cook for 2–3 minutes until just set.

3 Cook the second side for 35–45 seconds. Transfer to a plate and keep warm while you cook the remaining batter in the same way. (You should make about 16 pancakes in total.)

4 To serve, divide the pancakes among four warmed plates, piling them up in a stack. Drizzle honey over each stack and top with a dollop of yogurt.

Energy 373Kcal/1569kJ; Protein 11.2g; Carbohydrate 51.5g, of which sugars 23g; Fat 15.2g, of which saturates 7.8g; Cholesterol 172mg; Calcium 166mg; Fibre 2.1g; Sodium 161mg.

CARAMELIZED PLUMS WITH COCONUT RICE

RED, JUICY PLUMS ARE QUICKLY SEARED IN A WOK WITH SUGAR TO MAKE A RICH CARAMEL COATING, THEN SERVED WITH STICKY COCONUT-FLAVOURED RICE FOR A SATISFYING DESSERT. THE GLUTINOUS RICE IS AVAILABLE FROM ASIAN STORES, BUT REMEMBER THAT YOU HAVE TO SOAK IT OVERNIGHT.

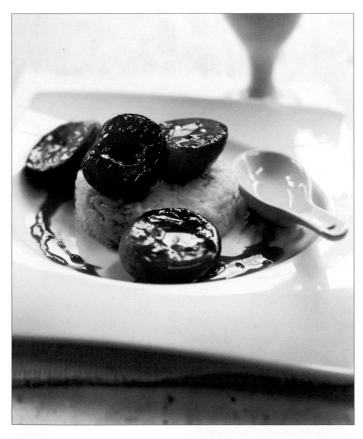

SERVES FOUR

INGREDIENTS
  6 or 8 firm, ripe plums
  90g/3½oz/½ cup caster
    (superfine) sugar
For the rice
  115g/4oz sticky glutinous rice
  150ml/¼ pint/⅔ cup coconut cream
  45ml/3 tbsp caster (superfine) sugar
  a pinch of salt

1 First prepare the rice. Rinse it in several changes of water, then leave to soak overnight in a bowl of cold water.

2 Line a large bamboo steamer that will fit in your wok with muslin (cheesecloth). Drain the rice and transfer it to the lined steamer.

3 Cover the rice and steam over simmering water for 25–30 minutes, until the rice is tender. (Check the water level and add more if necessary.)

4 Transfer the steamed rice to a wide bowl and set aside for a moment.

5 Combine the coconut cream with the sugar and salt and pour into a clean wok. Heat gently and bring to the boil, then remove from the heat and pour over the rice. Stir to mix well.

6 Using a sharp knife, cut the plums in half and remove their stones (pits). Sprinkle the sugar over the cut sides.

7 Heat a non-stick wok over a medium-high flame. Working in batches, place the plums in the wok, cut side down, and cook for 1–2 minutes, or until the sugar caramelizes. You may need to wipe out the wok with kitchen paper in between batches.

8 Mould the rice into rounds and place on warmed plates, then spoon over the caramelized plums. Alternatively, simply spoon the rice into four warmed bowls and top with the plums. Drizzle any syrup remaining in the wok over and around the fruit.

VARIATION
Try this with greengages. They look very pretty when piled on the discs of sticky rice. Red plums taste good if you add just a touch of balsamic vinegar to the syrup on serving.

Energy 298Kcal/1265kJ; Protein 3.6g; Carbohydrate 71.7g, of which sugars 50.2g; Fat 0.7g, of which saturates 0.1g; Cholesterol 0mg; Calcium 53mg; Fibre 2.4g; Sodium 47mg.

CARAMELIZED PINEAPPLE WITH LEMON GRASS

*THIS STUNNING DESSERT, GARNISHED WITH JEWEL-LIKE POMEGRANATE SEEDS, IS SUPERB FOR
ENTERTAINING. THE TANGY, ZESTY FLAVOURS OF LEMON GRASS AND MINT BRING OUT THE EXQUISITE
SWEETNESS OF THE PINEAPPLE TO CREATE A TRULY LUSCIOUS COMBINATION.*

SERVES FOUR

INGREDIENTS

    30ml/2 tbsp very finely chopped
      lemon grass, and 2 lemon grass
      stalks, halved lengthways
    350g/12oz/1¾ cups caster
      (superfine) sugar
    10ml/2 tsp chopped fresh mint
      leaves
    2 small, ripe pineapples, about
      600g/1lb 5oz each
    15ml/1 tbsp sunflower oil
    60ml/4 tbsp pomegranate seeds
    crème fraîche, to serve

1 Place the chopped lemon grass,
250g/9oz of the sugar and the mint
leaves in a non-stick wok. Pour over
150ml/¼ pint/⅔ cup of water and bring
to the boil over medium heat.

2 Reduce the heat under the wok and
simmer the mixture for 10–15 minutes,
until thickened. Strain into a glass bowl,
reserving the halved lemon grass stalks,
then set aside.

3 Using a sharp knife, peel and core
the pineapples and cut into 1cm/½in-
thick slices, then sprinkle the slices
with the remaining sugar.

4 Brush a large non-stick wok with the
oil and place over a medium heat.
Working in batches, cook the sugared
pineapple slices for 2–3 minutes until
they are lightly caramelised, then turn
over and cook the other side for another
2–3 minutes.

5 Transfer the pineapple slices to a
flat serving dish and scatter over the
pomegranate seeds.

6 Pour the lemon grass syrup over
the fruit and garnish with the reserved
stalks. Serve hot or at room temperature
with crème fraîche.

COOK'S TIP
To remove pomegranate seeds, halve
the fruit and hold it over a bowl, cut
side down. Tap all over with a wooden
spoon and the seeds should drop out.

Energy 493Kcal/2101kJ; Protein 1.6g; Carbohydrate 121.7g, of which sugars 121.7g; Fat 3.4g, of which saturates 0.3g; Cholesterol 0mg; Calcium 101mg; Fibre 3.6g; Sodium 11mg.

VANILLA, HONEY AND SAFFRON PEARS

THESE SWEET JUICY PEARS, POACHED IN A HONEY SYRUP INFUSED WITH VANILLA, SAFFRON AND LIME, MAKE A TRULY ELEGANT DESSERT. FOR A LOW-FAT VERSION YOU CAN EAT THEM ON THEIR OWN, BUT FOR A REALLY LUXURIOUS, INDULGENT TREAT, SERVE WITH CREAM OR ICE CREAM.

SERVES FOUR

INGREDIENTS
   150g/5oz/¾ cup caster
    (superfine) sugar
   105ml/7 tbsp clear honey
   5ml/1 tsp finely grated lime rind
   a large pinch of saffron
   2 vanilla pods (beans)
   4 large, firm ripe dessert pears
   single (light) cream or ice cream,
    to serve

COOK'S TIP
For the best results use firm varieties of dessert pears, such as comice or conference, that are well ripened.

1 Place the caster sugar and honey in a medium, non-stick wok, then add the lime rind and the saffron. Using a small, sharp knife, split the vanilla pods in half and scrape the seeds into the wok, then add the vanilla pods as well.

2 Pour 500ml/17fl oz/scant 2¼ cups water into the wok and bring the mixture to the boil. Reduce the heat to low and simmer, stirring occasionally, while you prepare the pears.

3 Peel the pears, then add to the wok and gently turn in the syrup to coat evenly. Cover the wok and simmer gently for 12–15 minutes, turning the pears halfway through cooking, until they are just tender.

4 Lift the pears from the syrup using a slotted spoon and transfer to four serving bowls. Set aside.

5 Bring the syrup back to the boil and cook gently for about 10 minutes, or until reduced and thickened. Spoon the syrup over the pears and serve either warm or chilled with single cream or ice cream.

COOK'S TIP
You can try using different flavourings in the syrup. Use 10ml/2 tsp chopped fresh root ginger and 1 or 2 star anise in place of the saffron and vanilla, or 1 cinnamon stick, 3 cloves and 105ml/ 7 tbsp maple syrup in place of the spices and honey. If the syrup seems too sweet for your taste, sharpen it with a little lemon or lime juice.

Energy 283Kcal/1207kJ; Protein 0.8g; Carbohydrate 74.3g, of which sugars 74.3g; Fat 0.2g, of which saturates 0g; Cholesterol 0mg; Calcium 38mg; Fibre 3.3g; Sodium 10mg.

INDEX